Beerbohm Tree's Olivia

Beerbohm Tree's
Olivia

by

Olivia Truman

Introduced and Edited
by her daughter
Isolde Wigram

ANDRE DEUTSCH

First published 1984 by
André Deutsch Limited
105 Great Russell Street London WC1

British Library Cataloguing in Publication Data
Truman, Olivia
    Beerbohm Tree's Olivia.
    I. Tree, Sir Herbert Beerbohm   2. Truman,
    Olivia   3. Theatre – England – Biography
    I. Title   II. Wigram, Isolde
    792'.092'4   PN2598.T7

ISBN 0-233-97702-3

1003988414 T

Photoset by Rowland Phototypesetting Ltd
Bury St Edmunds, Suffolk
and printed in Great Britain by
St Edmundsbury Press
Bury St Edmunds, Suffolk

Contents

List of Illustrations

* These pictures belong to The Raymond Mander and Joe Mitchenson Theatre Collection and are used with their kind permission. The remaining pictures are from Miss Wigram's own collection.

Introduction

In 1900, when she was twelve years old, my mother Olivia fell in love with the great actor manager Herbert Beerbohm Tree. The first ardent fan letter she sent him – 'I am thirteen and never loved so passionately before' – predictably drew no response but Olivia was not easily discouraged. She wrote again. She even sought an ally in Tree's half-brother, Max Beerbohm (whom she did not know either), and before long her devotion, which was to last until Tree's death in 1917, was rewarded. Tree's early letters to her reveal his reluctance to encourage such an unsuitable relationship. Not only was he the same age as her own mother but he was a married man with three daughters* and, as Olivia was later to discover, he had a second family in Putney where his mistress, May Pinney,† was bringing up six more of his children. Nothing of this, however, could overcome Olivia's conviction that she and Tree were destined for each other and though at first she was furiously jealous of his wife she could later write: 'Maud Tree and I met on several occasions and she was always very nice to me, though I had no doubt that she classed me as one of her husband's mistresses . . .' She also recorded that when Tree died Maud wrote: 'Herbert spoke of you so much and loved the flowers and things you sent him. I know you grieve for him and understand my grief.' The same generosity of spirit infused Olivia's later friendship with May Pinney whom Tree would surely have married had he been born a few years later when divorce, which he had certainly contemplated, had become more common.

Thirteen years after Tree's death, in 1930, Olivia went on a sort of pilgrimage to Marienbad, the health resort he used to visit annually, where she felt his spirit so close to her that she described it as a kind of spiritual honeymoon. It was here, as a tribute to him, that she incorporated his letters into an account of their unique relationship. She called the book *Beerbohm*

---

* Viola, Felicity and Iris. Their mother was the actress Maud Tree, née Holt.
† May Pinney later took the name 'Reed'. One of her sons was the film director Carol Reed. Oliver Reed, the actor, is one of her grandchildren.

Tree's Olivia but I do not know if she made any attempt to get it published at that time. During the late 1950s, when she was about seventy, she expanded it into a full-length autobiography, but was unable to get permission to publish all the Tree letters and abandoned the project some time before her death in 1970.

My own interest in the book was revived when I read Madeleine Bingham's *The Great Lover*, a biography of Tree, in 1978. She had found no trace of my mother's role in Tree's life, so I wrote to her telling her of this. In the meantime I had rediscovered in the attic a mass of letters which Olivia wrote to her one-time governess and confidante, Miss Mackay, during the whole period of her relationship with Tree, and which Miss Mackay, I think at Olivia's request, had returned to her to serve as a diary. With Madeleine Bingham's enthusiastic support, I therefore began to assemble the present book, abandoning the second part of the autobiography after Tree's death, and expanding the first part (which drew heavily on that original manuscript) by incorporating Olivia's own letters where they cover the events narrated in the text. I have also thought fit to preface *Beerbohm Tree's Olivia* with the opening pages of the autobiography, which describe Olivia's background and early years. They paint a vivid picture of a late Victorian childhood in which solid bourgeois virtues (and, by a strange coincidence, one side of Olivia's family, like Tree's own, was of Hanseatic stock) were enlivened by quite startling aberrations. The reader will learn that both my grandfather and great-grandfather had lasting relationships with ladies other than their wives. No wonder Olivia was so tolerant of the confusion of women in Tree's life.

One family mentioned in the letters needs clarification: the Alexanders. Olivia got to know this family when staying with her grandparents in Sussex and they were her closest childhood companions. Lady Emily Alexander (a daughter of the Earl of Cork) was the mother, and the children were Ulick (who later held the office of the King's Privy Purse), Evelyn, Olivia's close friend and contemporary who died soon after her marriage, Jacqueline, known as 'Cockie', and a younger boy, Cedric.

Finally, I would like to acknowledge the help of Mr Kenneth McClellan in selecting the Mackay letters, and above all the generous encouragement of Madeleine Bingham.

A word about the presentation: my own commentary appears throughout in italics. I have kept this and all critical apparatus to a minimum. The vibrant spelling and punctuation in Olivia's letters (which become more regular but never quite correct as she grows up) are her own.

Olivia's daughter Isolde

Prologue

Extract from Olivia Truman's unpublished autobiography describing her childhood up to the onset of that passionate attachment which is the subject of the book that follows.

On 11 April 1888 at 32 Hans Place, Knightsbridge, a baby girl was born to Colonel and Mrs Truman.

The address and parentage were respectable rather than distinguished; I have done my best to become more distinguished, without much success, and in the process have become less respectable.

My father, ex-Colonel of the 5th and 7th Dragoon Guards, later to become Inspector General of Remounts, was collaterally descended from Mrs Montagu of Bluestocking fame, who had been a Miss Robinson. A relative of hers, another Robinson, seems to have been an heiress and to have compromised herself with a young man from the West Country called Samuel Truman. Whether it was a case of true love or whether he thought her fortune was an easy way of improving his own I do not know, but their marriage resulted in the family to which my father belonged. His own father was a doctor, who must have been a somewhat peculiar man, for, after marrying and having several children, he disappeared to Italy for about ten years, after which he turned up again, settled down with his wife, and continued to supply her with babies! Both he and my grandmother, who looks a plain woman, died before I was born, and as my father was on bad terms with most of his relations, I never heard anything about them.

My mother was of German blood, her father and mother coming over here from Hamburg soon after their marriage. From the portraits of their forbears they seem to have been of prosperous Hanseatic stock. My grandfather set up as a general merchant, which I take it means that he bought up anything that was going cheap and sold it dear, which he did with such success that at one period his income was £25,000 a year at an epoch when that represented three times what it does now. He died worth a quarter of a million.

He had great political foresight, but inspired little affection, being very much the Teutonic bully. My grandmother must have been a lovely woman, judging by Desanges's painting of her, but unresponsive to her husband's marital ardours, with the result that he transferred them to a lady in Kensington, silencing my grandmother's protests with gifts of diamonds, of which she gained a good display, now unhappily long 'gone up the spout'. My mother was their only child, and adored of her father. He was a keen rider to hounds, and from extreme youth she followed him in the hunting fields of the Midland packs; she was also his companion at the Opera, of which as a true German he was a devotee. As she was a considerable heiress, and a good-looking girl, her parents hoped for a brilliant marriage for her. The Prince de Chimay did indeed propose to her, but she found him ridiculous, and became engaged to an Irish peer. This romance was ended by a quarrel, and on the rebound, she accepted my father, a rather impecunious lieutenant in the 13th Hussars. They were married at St James's, Piccadilly, my grandfather imploring her, to the last, to change her mind. Their honeymoon was spent at Cowes and Mother seems to have amused herself rolling a tin bath down the stairs of the hotel – it was the era of very infantile practical jokes.

In due course she gave birth to a boy, Harry, who died of meningitis at Cannes before I was born. Later came my brothers, Ivor and Charles, nine and seven years my senior. My grandfather had stipulated that my father should leave the 13th Hussars, who were due to go to India, and he had therefore joined the 5th Dragoons. When my brothers were still quite small, my father was offered command of the 7th Dragoons, who were on the verge of being disbanded for lack of discipline. They were already in India, and this time my grandfather consented to my mother accompanying her husband there, leaving the boys with their grandmother. Mother travelled out in the same ship as the new Viceroy, Lord Dufferin, with whom she made great friends, much to her advantage, as he accorded her many privileges on her arrival. She always told me he was one of the most charming men she ever met. At first she hated India, where she remained two years, but later settled down, and seems to have had a fabulously good time. She never spoke of any duties in connection with the Regiment, but of endless house parties at the palaces of Residents and Rajahs. It was the period of Kipling's *Plain Tales from the Hills* and enlivened with very sultry scandals.

When she eventually sailed for home she preceded my father by some months, and had the misfortune to be shipwrecked off Corsica. The passengers escaped in their nightwear, having to make their way over rocks which cut their feet badly. My mother was assisted by a friend, the Earl of Buckinghamshire, who was subsequently photographed in the clothes he wore on that occasion – a very loud check coat and a deerstalker hat . . . My mother was taller than most women of her generation and had difficulty in being fitted out, until garments arrived from England. No previous P & O ship having ever foundered, her belongings, including some fine jewellery, were not insured, so that she sustained a considerable loss. The divers retrieved her jewel case – empty.

I always assign my advent to my father's emotion at seeing my mother again after her escape from this adventure. It could not have been intentional, as it made their charming little house in Hans Place too small for them and they were obliged to move. My eldest brother having been kicked by a pony and developed internal abscesses, they were advised to take him to the sea, and went to live at Folkestone, where I think they remained for two years. I believe it was there that my father met a lady who continued to attract him for the rest of his life.

My grandparents had now bought an estate between Eridge and Crowborough, with a large house of almost unbelievable ugliness – an Italian villa with a basement, copied by its previous owner from one in St John's Wood. My mother protested in vain against its purchase, and refused to have it bequeathed to her. Yet with all its lack of beauty, I look back to my life there with nostalgia. It stood in a commanding position, with a lovely view across the Sussex landscape which is always dearest to my heart, and which means 'England' to me. Its grounds had paths winding through great rhododendrons, and nut thickets, and included towering rocks, bearing the marks of the period when they were sea-washed, and in them caves said to be used by smugglers. It had three farms, the Home one, managed by a bailiff whose wife came from Devonshire and who made cowslip wine – a very nectar of the Gods to me – cream cheeses, and junkets flavoured with brandy, and covered with an unbroken richness of golden clotted cream from the big pans standing in the dairy. Then there was the high-walled kitchen garden, where next to the laundry was the store house of the orchard's produce carefully laid out on straw on shelves. Pears and apples have never tasted like those bestowed on me there by the old Scots gardener. There were also the stables with their boxes and stalls filled with large fat horses, and their coachhouses with a variety of vehicles – phaetons, landaus, wagonettes, victorias, broughams, dog-carts, pony-carts – above which assortment dwelt the coachman, a real period piece with mutton-chop whiskers.

Most wondrous of all was the range of glasshouses, where vines, peaches, nectarines, and early strawberries grew – Maréchal Niel roses fanned overhead, and the smilax* which was *sine qua non* of Victorian dinner tables. Then there was the moist heat of the tropical house with orchids, and

* A decorative plant.

fly-catching plants cupping a gruesome collection of dead bodies, and the 'sensitive' plant which folded up when touched, and of course lots and lots of maidenhair fern. Melons and cucumbers hung in nets in a house of their own.

Somewhere near the glasshouses I had my own garden, always suffering from under- or over-watering, where I loved to pop my little fingers in and out of the snapdragons (only later did they become antirrhinums!) and smell the sweetpeas with little flowers possessing a perfume so exquisite that none of their large descendants can atone for its loss. A little frightening was the cement reservoir, intended for ornament but ugly, always half full of water and containing newts and other creatures which disgusted me. Last there was the pond on which my grandfather spent vast sums, but which would never retain water and is long dried up – but at times one could actually row or punt about it, and even skate on it in winter. I can see myself now in a double-breasted red jacket, a white silk handkerchief carefully crossed round my throat, being tugged across the ice by my two brothers.

Within what was referred to by the tenants as 'the Mansion' all that was worst in Victorian taste – or lack of it – abounded. The drawing room was a riot of plush curtains with deep fringes, Sèvres clocks, small silver ornaments, Venetian chandeliers. It opened on to a magnificent winter garden, chock-a-block with palms, where at Christmas a giant tree soared to the roof. The employees and their children stood obsequiously round this, to receive the presents which had been accumulated in an upstairs room for weeks previously. My grandparents being German took Christmas very seriously and certainly did it regally. Across the hallway the walls of the dining room were decorated with brilliantly coloured oil paintings of Norway, which looked down on the long table loaded with food (though my grandmother often declared there was nothing to eat) and my grandfather disposing of a brace of hock on his own. My nurseries were on the second floor – their dun-coloured wallpaper dimly lit by one of the earliest electrical installations, generated in a power house in the grounds, where the huge fly wheel and driving belt terrified me, and which was presided over by a little whiskered gnome of a man who might have been own cousin to Mime!*

I remember every detail of the two rooms which I shared with my nurse: as I drifted off to sleep the night-light shadowing the framed presentation plates on the walls – 'Bubbles', 'Cherry Ripe', Queen Alexandra (as she became) lovely in a black chiffon dress, clasping a bunch of red roses. In the day nursery the piano with its fretwork front, the big centre table carrying the home-made cakes, scones and jams of a real old-fashioned tea, and below it an outsize Noah's ark. The dancing fire behind the high guard, the mantel

* The evil dwarf in Wagner's *Siegfried*.

draped with red serge bob-fringed, and displaying an assortment of small ornaments. The rocking chair, my dolls' furniture and grocer's shop. How ugly – how comfortable – how happy!

When not at Eridge my grandparents inhabited a beautiful house in Gloucester Terrace, Regent's Park. It was the palace of a merchant prince, resplendent in crimson silk damask, gilt and marble, and more pictures of the worst taste. Anyone acquainted with that period of domestic architecture will know how it was built for show, with a fine stone staircase flanked by gilt wrought-iron, sweeping up to a suite of reception rooms on the first floor, and then disappearing through a hidden door on to the steep and dreary approach to the bedroom regions. My nurseries were, of course, on the top landing and commanded a wide view of the park towards the zoo whence the roaring of the lions could be heard, often to my great alarm lest it preluded their escape. The house swarmed with domestics, the junior ones doomed to lug coals, and hot water for the hip baths, up the endless flights of steps.

In the lordly dining room banquets took place attended by various German relatives, large-bosomed ladies, respectable in lace caps and bodices tightly buttoned up to their necks. Fat, unfortunately, runs in both sides of my family – the wife of my grandfather's twin brother could easily have appeared as an exhibit at a fair.

My mother used to tell me of the dinner parties of her youth, when my grandfather handed out ten pounds for the dessert alone, and the gold plate was solemnly fetched from the bank. When my grandmother died no trace could be found of this and it remains an unsolved problem – was she perhaps short of cash at some period of her widowhood? – or did the butler get away with it?

My grandfather died when I was only five, but I remember him fairly clearly: a large man with spectacles and mutton-chop whiskers – very irascible. He used to take me driving in his mail phaeton whilst in Sussex, shouting abuse at anyone who dared to use the roads at the same moment.

In London the daily routine included an outing with my grandmother in the barouche, the most regal of conveyances, drawn by two of the large fat horses and conducted by the ancient coachman whom my grandmother always accused of 'racing with the buses'. It seemed quite an expedition from Gloucester Terrace to Marshall and Snelgrove's in Oxford Street, which was generally our destination, so that my grandmother might add yet another jet-loaded velvet or satin garment to her collection. When she died her bill there amounted to hundreds of pounds.

I have little recollection of my early life with my parents. When I was three my mother took me to France for six months, and we lived at the Hotel des Reservoirs at Versailles, later to become famous as the hotel used by the peace delegations in 1918. I used to play at the Petit Trianon, and drink milk hot from the cows there. A gourmet from the earliest age, though I had been a poor eater in England, I ate the French food with gusto! I was a naughty child, given to such fits of rage that I would throw myself on the ground and roar but my mother would never allow my nurses to give me the good whipping I deserved, with the result none of them would remain with me, except a dear old lady who had looked after me for a time at Folkestone. She was eventually recalled and stayed with me till I was twelve. She belonged to the old order of devoted domestics, with her white aprons and caps, and neat little outdoor bonnet. She never seemed to have a holiday, or even a day out, her only recreations being tea and gossip. Her father had been a Manchester school-master, I imagine of Evangelical views, as she instilled into me the wicked-ness of sewing on Sunday, and the sinfulness of my mother's use of lipstick, then of course only worn by rather go-ahead ladies, the very slightest application (in secret) of powder being as far as the really chaste might venture. I used to pray to the Almighty to rescue my erring parent from the fires which awaited her if she continued on this path.

The period between our visit to France and our settling in Beaufort Gardens, Brompton Road, when I was about seven, is nearly a blank to me, though I *do* remember a flat in Queen Anne's Mansions, and a dreadful little semi-detached house on the main road near Maidenhead Bridge, which we had the year of the marriage of King George and Queen Mary (then Duke and Duchess of York) – of 'Ta-ra-ra-boom-di-ay' and 'A bicycle built for two' – of ladies with enormous sleeves and frizzy fringes à la Princesse de Galles which were often removable (sometimes involuntarily so) and 'switches' of hair to make the 'teapot handles' on top of the head.

From then on every detail becomes clear. The houses in that cul-de-sac (Beaufort Gardens), then as now, were high, ugly Victorian buildings, the Brompton Road was still somewhat squalid and Harrods quite a small general store. The streets were lit by gas, hence a lamplighter going his rounds at dusk, there were muffin men and 'German bands', men in peaked caps who stood in the street in circles vigorously blowing their brass instruments in competition with flunkeys and parlourmaids whistling hansoms and four-wheelers to take ladies with low-cut dresses revealing overflowing bosoms above tightly compressed waists, and gentlemen in high collars and starched shirts, to dinner parties and theatres. It was the London where Society was still spelt with a capital S and its scandals recorded in a dreadful little weekly paper avidly read and hastily concealed under sofa cushions. The Prince of Wales's amours supplied plenty of copy, and there were fearfully naughty plays like *The Second Mrs Tanqueray* and *The Doll's House* that could not be mentioned before young persons. Oscar Wilde scintillated at the Café Royal,

Max Beerbohm was a literary lion with the roar of a sucking dove, Sargent sparred with Whistler . . .

Of this social background I was, as yet, more or less ignorant – in fact I was ignorant of a great deal more than that, for I still could not even read – principally, I think, because I was too lazy, and my old nurse did nothing to remedy this, foolishly continuing to read aloud to me. No one at that time, or ever, really bothered about my education which has always remained sadly lacking. A dear old lady did indeed arrive and make some attempt to begin my instruction, but except for memorising 'The Inchcape Rock', I learned nothing, and she abandoned the uneven contest. She was succeeded by an Alsatian who had been governess to some friends, but beyond making us intimately acquainted with the affairs of her late employers, I do not think she achieved much else – anyhow I still could not read. Eventually, I picked it up fast enough, when a new teacher at Totland Bay (we had taken a cottage at Yarmouth for a winter, I don't know why) started me on a story in which I became interested and refused to finish it for me.

There is no doubt that, if I lacked book learning, I knew a great deal about things I should have been better without. Both my brothers being so much older than I, I lived as practically an only child, was terribly spoilt, and passed far too much time with grown-up people.

I was of course garbed in the extraordinary clothes in which children of that time were encased, combinations, flannel petticoats, long stockings, high-laced boots, and elaborate party dresses with high collars. I remember a grey velvet with a lilac yoke, and one of bottle green velvet with a torquoise yoke edged with fur, and long sleeves! There is a photo of me in a garden at the age of nine, in frilly muslin with a wide sash, with a chiffon hat decorated with ostrich feathers!

That was the year we took a house in Abingdon for the summer, where after dinner one night the party were sitting out in the darkness exchanging yarns, quite oblivious of my presence, until I chipped in with the electrifying remark 'I know a much more disgusting story than that!' What it was did not eventuate. I was indeed an *enfant terrible*. My mother never heard the last of the occasion when, in playing a charade of a mistress and a cook, I instructed the latter to send up the second-class champagne well iced as the people who were coming were not very important . . .

My mother amused herself with gambling on the Stock Exchange and, but for the Jameson Raid,* would have made a considerable fortune; this development, which her father with his political flair might have foreseen

* The Jameson Raid, which provoked the Boer War, was in support of foreigners speculating in the newly discovered gold mines who were prevented from getting their money out by swingeing taxes imposed by South Africa's President Kruger.

Prologue

had he lived, cost her all she had made and a great deal more. Anyhow, there was much talk of 'Johnnies' and 'de Beers', etc., in my presence, and the comings and goings of various other speculators, some interested in similar ventures, others in paying court to my mother, who was still a handsome woman with a great liking for and attraction for the male sex.

My father's military duties often took him from home, and my memories of him are neither very clear nor very affectionate. Besides being a first-rate judge of a horse, he was a very good shot, had charming manners, and was popular with a wide acquaintance. He owned a great many clothes, and innumerable boots, and on Sundays often used to review his wardrobe.

I cannot remember anyone very interesting or distinguished coming to the house, my impression is that our friends were respectable and dull. Of course we had dinner parties – they were part of the convention – and I used to be paraded in the drawing room before the guests went downstairs and then often managed to hang round, and pick up delicacies on their way back to the kitchen. A chef used to be imported for these occasions. He ordered in a vast quantity of stores, and arrived with a bevy of pupils, who ate up or removed everything left over.

The table used to be spread with a damask cloth 'decorated' with a ghastly gold-embroidered satin centre piece, and trails of the inevitable smilax. The room itself showed no more taste, since my father had forbidden my mother to improve its original decoration . . . The staircase rioted in large peonies and was hung with prints of Morland's pictures. The drawing room, papered in sealing-wax red, boasted unsuitable cretonne covers, draped palms, shiny photos (including Lord Buckinghamshire in the deerstalker) and of course a 'silver table' of small trash. The balcony opening out of it and extending over the porch was tented over with a striped awning in summer, carpeted and furnished and coffee solemnly partaken of among the smuts, no doubt accompanied by the latest gossip as to the Prince's mistresses and the new Pinero, and (prior to Jameson) the price of Johnnies.

Above the drawing room was my mother's bedroom, an even worse horror with a paper of tea roses, and elaborately carved oak furniture stained black! My own bedroom opened out of it, with a similar paper, and furniture of light ash. Is it to be wondered at that I was a bad sleeper?

We had a domestic staff of four, apart from my nurse: cook, housemaid, 'between maid', and a manservant. The latter was generally of Latin origin, and demanded frequent replacements for having either stolen the wine and cigars, or spent the night out, or both. The lack of morals of the master was never allowed to the domestic. It was indeed a time of the stupidest taboos, when 'ladies' did not drive in omnibuses, nor respectable young girls in hansom cabs, nor could they go about with an open-throated dress – high

xviii

collars sustained by whalebones which left red marks on the neck were *de rigueur*, and to reverse while waltzing was very bad form!

In these surroundings, still tended by the faithful nurse, I continued until my twelfth year, for the last eighteen months attending a day school where my aptitude for history, biblical and secular, took me to the top of the class but failed to improve my spelling, arithmetic or grammar.

My parents then decided to move to Taplow* from whence my father could travel to London daily, to discharge his duty of finding horses for the use of the army in the Boer War. Poor man, he operated from a small flat in Victoria Street and it would have taken a far greater organiser than he was to cope with the situation, about which he had warned the War Office, in vain begging them to let him start buying before the storm broke. When it did he had to recruit assistants to send abroad as best he could, and without being able to check up on them sufficiently. A certain number proved dishonest, and at the end of the war he was held responsible for this, and an enquiry held. In the event he was personally exonerated but the worry affected his health which he never properly recovered. Matters were not improved by my second brother, Charles, who had joined the 12th Royal Lancers at the front, being court-martialled for joining in ragging a very undesirable man in Cape Town. He was lucky to escape being cashiered. These affairs, the seriousness of which I was too young to realise, left me uninterested. I hardly knew my brother, on account of his having been brought up by my grandmother (a thing he never forgave my mother), and I had been merely bored when taken to bid him farewell before he left for Africa. The worthy old lady simply doted on him, and to the last believed him to be a pattern of all the virtues, which he was very far indeed from being, but no one can blame her for falling victim to one of the most charming men I have ever known. In due course, a photograph of him in the elaborate full dress of his regiment joined the other shiny photos on the piano, larger and shinier than any of them.

The last year of the century saw us established at our new home, to which we moved whilst snow was on the ground, and the cold so great that I had to share my mother's bed for warmth. In a way the house was rather charming, with a central hall with a gallery running round it, from which opened the bedrooms, still furnished with beds of brass. Alas! the tasteless Victorian sideboard and chairs, and I suppose the satin centre pieces, still accompanied us, though the palms may have shed some of their draperies and the 'silver table' brought under control. I now boasted a 'schoolroom' in place of a nursery, and the faithful Nanny was replaced by a governess, to whom I quickly grew as much attached as she to me. During the all too short eighteen

* Near Maidenhead, but just over the Berkshire border, in Buckinghamshire.

months of her residence she gave me the only bit of sound educational grounding I ever had. She wooed me to conjugate French verbs by allowing me to study them on the fender stool whilst we made toast and brewed cocoa; she struggled valiantly to overcome my incurable inability to spell, with daily dictations. She allowed me to translate La Rochefoucauld's *Maxims* as a means of learning French. She even copied out the astonishing results of my early attempts at authorship. When I was barely nine and could neither spell nor write legibly, I had begun with paraphrasing the poetry of Tennyson which my mother was given to reading aloud. I believed that intense melancholy was the mark of maturity, and though an extremely cheerful child, I composed 'verses' on the lines of the following:

> I am sad,
> For we are sad
> And all we see around is sad and dreary
> And my heart is weary
> Lingering on this river of life
> Like a sunbeam on the dark water
> We sway like vessels in a storm
> And sink never to rise again
> Oh! death! why do you linger so long
> Oh! take me away
> That I may have rest and peace for aye. *

These 'poems' written on odd scraps of paper were followed by stories, whose humour compares with *The Young Visiters*. The first dealt with an elopement to Gretna in a balloon . . . the next with an heiress, whose parents have refused to consent to her marriage with a poor man . . . but all ends happily when he inherits 'a treasure worth several million' which naturally causes her family to take a more favourable view of him. By the time we went to Taplow I had embarked on a very lurid story of crime called *The World, the Flesh and the Devil* which our old gardener described as a combination of all the penny dreadfuls he had read during the last twenty years. And that is about what it was, for my reading, when I had at last mastered it, seems to have been quite uncensored, ranging from Henty, Fergus Hume, Dick Donovan, down to the Penny Pictorial.

Such then was the child who, having finished the French verbs, the toast and the cocoa, took up her pen, and, adding a year to her age, wrote in her unspeakable orthography to the great actor manager of Her Majesty's Theatre – 'I am thirteen and never loved so passionately before.' This amazing

* I can give no idea of the actual spelling [Olivia's note].

declaration, worthy of a George Sand or a Cora Pearl at the height of their *vie d'amour*, was, perhaps, somewhat of an overstatement. My previous heroes had been a Red Indian in a series of boys' adventure books; the Reverend Storrs, then vicar of St Peter's, Eaton Square, and a short-lived and not very ardent attachment to Sir Pertob Singh who had caught my fancy when he rode in the procession at Queen Victoria's Diamond Jubilee.

For many Sundays I used to attend St Peter's, and await the delicious moment when my clerical idol would mount the pulpit, and give out the text of his sermon in his rich Irish brogue. At length I made the great discovery that a friend's stepfather was acquainted with this paragon. I prevailed on him to arrange an interview with him in the vestry after the service, but as the moment drew near, my courage began to ebb. Brought face to face with him in the austere atmosphere of vestments and sacramental wine, it deserted me wholly, and I beat a hasty retreat. It is probably the only occasion on which audacity has failed me completely . . .

Beerbohm Tree's

Olivia

Publisher's Note

In order to retain the full flavour of Olivia's letters the publisher has not interfered with her breathless punctuation and erratic spelling. Dates and addresses, where they existed, have been retained when they seemed interesting or helpful. Omissions – whether of a sentence or several paragraphs – have been indicated by one set of ellipses. Occasionally, in the interests of legibility, a page-length paragraph has been broken up and, in the interests of space, short paragraphs have sometimes been run together. Isolde's commentary appears in italics. Her annotations of her mother's text appear as footnotes to the narrative and as interpolations in the letters. The authors of all plays mentioned in the text can be found by reference to the index.

1901-1904

The event that was to influence my entire life had no dramatic prelude. The name of Beerbohm Tree meant nothing to me – I do not think that the theatre was ever seriously discussed in our household, though my mother used often to go to plays. She saw *Captain Swift* not long before I was born, little imagining that the leading actor would ever come into her life. I remember one day when I was with her in a hansom, and we were driving along Pall Mall, she pointed to a man in one coming towards us, and said 'That is Tree.' It is significant that his pale face and worried expression remained in my memory. Just before we left London a friend took me to see *A Midsummer Night's Dream* at Her Majesty's – and *what* a dream it was with Julia Neilson as Oberon, Louie Freer as Puck, Gerald Lawrence, Lewis Waller, Dorothea Baird and Sarah Brook as the lovers. But it was not the famous matinée idol,* for all his handsome looks and his gold armour, who caught my attention: it was the grotesquely made up Bottom with his blob nose and hairy legs – Herbert Beerbohm Tree.

There is one belief that I have never wavered in, however many others have come and gone, and that is Reincarnation, without which life seems to me to lack either sense or justice. It is the key of all the mysteries: it explains quite simply why, when a child of twelve heard a man of forty-five speak, she recognised him she was to love for always.

It was however one thing for a child of twelve, having no links with the artistic world, to nourish a passion for a middle-aged and famous actor, and quite another to attract his attention. I began in the orthodox manner by writing to request his autograph, but so much was I enmeshed in the conventions of my kind that I thought it improper to use my own name, and gave a pseudonym, and the address of a friend. From that moment Fate took a hand. I wrote to warn the friend that a letter with the *nom de plume* might arrive, and asking her to forward it, but she was away from home. Tree

* Lewis Waller, who is to reappear in this story as the constant escort of Mrs Tree.

answered, and when she returned she found that his letter had been refused by the servants. When I learned this I was beside myself with disappointment, and casting the proprieties recklessly away, wrote to him again, explaining the situation, and signing my own name. Had I received the original letter what would then have occurred? Should I ever have written to him again? – and on what pretext? – or would I have let 'concealment like a worm i' the bud feed on my damask cheek'? Vain speculation, I suppose, for I was born to come into his life.

This time I drew no response, and I was utterly disconsolate. We were now established at Taplow, and my dear governess, Miss Mackay, was made the confidante of this tragic love affair. She was as sympathetic to that as to my literary efforts. The *Midsummer Night's Dream* had been in January. In the spring Tree put on *Rip Van Winkle* to which my grandmother was persuaded to escort me – I had a remarkable gift for coaxing people to aid and abet me in the most unlikely way. As Rip restored to youth Tree was more the sort of man to attract a girl, with his height, his fair hair, blue eyes, and Teutonic good looks. My temperature responded accordingly, but it was not until the autumn – October 10th to be exact – when I saw him as Mark Antony in a revival of his magnificent production of *Julius Caesar* that I reached boiling point, and wrote him the historic words 'I am thirteen and never loved so passionately before.'

No doubt I expected that Her Majesty's Theatre would rock to its foundations when its owner read this tremendous announcement. Alas! there was no repercussion at all. I was left to my French verbs, my dictation and my cocoa without a ray of hope. I wrote again, still without eliciting a reply. It was not until I had the brilliant idea of asking him for a subscription to the funds of the S.S.F.A., for which I was collecting (the Boer War was in progress), that I at long last received a letter from him:

28 June 1901   Her Majesty's Theatre

My dear Miss Truman,

     I have great pleasure in sending you a cheque for two guineas for the Soldiers and Sailors Families. I hope you will be most successful in your collection. I remain,

Yours sincerely,
Herbert Beerbohm Tree

My joy knew no bounds. In my hands I actually held the paper he had touched, the words he had penned! A little formal perhaps, ignoring all the outpourings of my love, but still from him! It of course necessitated an immediate and lengthy acknowledgement; I suspect followed by several others without excuse, and apparently by floral offerings. Then one August day (1901) my mother brought me up an envelope bearing a foreign postmark: it was from him, from Marienbad. It ran:

July 23   Gruenes Kreuz,* Marienbad, Austria

Dear Miss Truman,
        I have been intending to write to you for some time, firstly, to thank you for your kindness in sending me those pretty gifts of fruit and flowers, and secondly, to beg you not to send any more, for I am sure you can spend your pocket money much more profitably.
        Please do not think me ungracious, and indeed I am greatly touched by your kind thought of me.
        In a former letter you gave me to understand that you had withheld it from your parents that I had sent you a cheque for your Widows' and Orphans' Fund. I think you ought at once to tell your mother that you had written to me and that I had responded to your request. I do not think it would be becoming, were I to write to you without her knowledge, and I am sure you will agree with me in this, and not think me churlish or priggish.
        Thanking you again for your interest in me, I remain, with best wishes for your happiness,

                                        Yours sincerely,
                                        Herbert Beerbohm Tree

P.S. In a former letter you mentioned something about Mrs Fagg [his sister-in-law] – will you kindly tell me if you know her. I should be so glad to know. H.B.T.

It is rather lonely here as I am almost the solitary Englishman and my family are at home.

Whether or not I should have done as he requested and informed my mother of what I had been up to, I know not, but the matter was decided for me by her demanding to know who had written to me from abroad, and when I feebly tried to lie, her insisting on seeing the letter. The cat was out of the bag, and I got a very stern lecture on the impropriety of my conduct, finishing with strict

* The Gruenes Kreuz was a large hotel much frequented by English visitors.

instructions to cease writing to him. I wept inconsolably, and made a series of grotesque entries in my diary – the only one I have ever kept. By this time I had made Tree into a cult. The recess in which stood my school desk was adorned with pictures of him in the plays in which I had seen him, and on the corner of the mantelpiece, whence he could overlook my struggles with French verbs and the rule of three, was a peculiarly bad photograph of him with a dog, looking rather bilious.

Further, on one occasion when in London – when or how I do not know – I had contrived to get to his house in Sloane Street, and to touch the spot on his front door where his hand would rest when using his latch-key, with my best pocket handkerchief (embroidered in blue and white clover leaves) which was then placed in an enamel casket! I ignored the fact that Mrs Tree must also use a latch-key, and the servant occasionally clean round the brasswork. No saint's relic was ever more cherished than this absurd handkerchief.

Everything was made to have some connection with him. My birds – a canary and a bullfinch – were named Rip Van Winkle and Herod; on the trees in the garden, and the pillars of its little temple, I carved his initials 'H.B.T.' Looking back I do not know how all this folly was permitted me, or how I managed to get regularly to his plays.

I know that he put on *Twelfth Night*, *Herod* and *Ulysses* all about this time. The first was particularly lovely and well acted, and his Malvolio one of his greatest creations. I went to it armed with a notebook and pencil in order that I could record the exact moment he came on, and made his exits, so that at home I could picture what he was doing at a given time. (I made no allowance for the inaccuracies of watches.) On the completion of its century he gave away a charming souvenir with coloured pictures of the scenes and performers, and delighted me by sending me one with his own portrait signed. This I immediately had framed, and one evening had arranged it on a table surrounded by lighted candles, altar form, and was contemplating it with all the ardour of a devotee before an icon, when I was interrupted by the entry of the housemaid, and made to feel extremely foolish. There was a curiously eastern touch in the homage I paid him.

I will spare readers all extracts, save one, from my diary, but in it I constantly refer to him in some such manner as 'the shining light from heaven', and I used to address him in writing to him as 'My Lord'. Believing in reincarnation I can only suppose that formerly I was his slave. I have always fancied that he must have been a Roman patrician. He had so much the Roman type of head, and one could picture him discoursing with his brilliant wit at one of the feasts of Epicurus, not perhaps unmindful of the beauty of the dancers and serving maids.

Not very long after my letter from Marienbad my mother was surprised to receive one from him, asking if she would spare him a few minutes' conversation at the theatre. Uncertain as to what he wanted, she consented, and to my unspeakable joy promised to let me accompany her. I went attired in my best coat and skirt of grey cloth, and a frilly pink silk hat rather like an elaborate strawberry ice, and felt painfully conscious of my youth – how difficult to make any man treat one seriously with skirts only reaching to one's knees, for maturity in those days demanded a yard or two of material sweeping the ground.

The rendezvous must have been after four o'clock in the hall at His Majesty's, for I know the lights were lit. My mother and I drove up in a hansom, in which I was left while she went inside. My emotion and excitement were so great that I could hardly contain them. Through the glass doors I could see into the vestibule, with its black and white marble floor and oak-panelled walls, adorned by a big oil painting of Tree as King John, a part in which, alas, I never saw him. Within a minute or two of my mother leaving me he came down the stairs leading to the foyer and dress circle with the quick light step I was to know so well. He wore the frock-coat and top hat that was then generally worn by men in London. Again I beheld the rounded pale face, the brilliant blue eyes, and the mobile mouth drooping to the left corner, of the man of the hansom cab – the reality behind Bottom, Rip, Mark Antony, Herod, Malvolio.

My heart almost stopped beating as I watched him greet my mother and stand in conversation with her. After a few moments that seemed like eternity, she turned and beckoned to me, and trembling from head to foot, still fully conscious of those short skirts, I climbed out of the cab and joined them. We shook hands, and neither of us could think of anything to say. My tongue was cleaving to the roof of my mouth, my knees nearly giving way under me. He stood regarding me, I expect rather embarrassed himself in the presence of a third party. My mother and he were almost exactly contemporaries: a dreadful gulf seemed suddenly to open between our generations. How hopeless to be passionately in love with one who might have been one's father! I remember little else; I think my mother, aware of our awkwardness, removed me quickly. That was our first meeting. Five years were to pass before I was to see him again.

I concluded my diary for 1901, most of which had been occupied with my maunderings about him, interspersed with the assassination of President McKinley, the death of Queen Victoria, and a game of bumble-puppy with Sir Evelyn Wood, in the following words:

The name of the man to whom I have given up my
whole year in this book is the last I wish to write.
For a whole year he has been my life. I close it
with his name on my lips. I pray heart and soul
that whatever I think of him, that God will bless
and protect him always and always, guide him in
every way, bless him with success and happiness, and
everlasting life(!!)   May I never be able to take
back this solemn prayer whatever I ever think of him,
I now make this an eternal blessing. So here closes
the first chapter of my life, my first love – my
love and the year die together, buried in my heart,
and the first and last words and thoughts I wrote
and think, and which will always have sweet memories
for me – the person I eternally commend to God are
and is

Herbert Beerbohm Tree!!

Alas for him, my passion did not perish so easily.

At the meeting with my mother, Tree seems merely to have wished to give
her his assurance that he was doing nothing to encourage my infatuation. But
no encouragement was needed: the more he stood off, the more ardent I
became.

I had one small lapse in the direction of an American actor called William
Gillette* whom I saw as Sherlock Holmes, and about whom I immediately
wrote a novel, crediting him with discovering a sister-in-law in the slums, and
educating her so successfully that within a few months she was able not only
to save the Prime Minister the trouble of writing the King's Speech by doing it
for him, but also to render a similar service in the matter of a sermon for the
Archbishop of Canterbury. Finally Mr Gillette was made to die in a duel in
the neighbourhood of Le Touquet in defence of the honour of this paragon.
But before my hero was decently buried I repented of my penchant for him
(though for some while I continued to copy his manner of crossing his t's) and
returned to what Herbert subsequently called my 'Tree habit'.

*This seems an appropriate point at which to insert the first of Olivia's letters to her
former governess and confidante, Miss Mackay (not the first that she wrote, but the*

---

* From whom Olivia must have received a letter or signed photograph.

first it is relevant to include here). She had just been to see Tree in Trilby, and this is the judgement of the fourteen-year-old Olivia, in her own spelling. The letter is dated June 25th, 1902.

. . . I went to 'Trilby' on Saturday, cold and all – nothing on earth could have kept me away, and oddly it made me no worse   it was Sunday I got it so bad. I enclose a paper on the play full of 'gass' and a programm, please be careful of the sacred articles and return at an early date. I have always adored Mr Tree because he was so soft and sweet and such a great artist, but I don't think I have ever really thought him an extraordainry actor beyond his versitility, till Saturday. Of the 9 plays I've seen him in, he has never played with the depth, the feeling, the power, the subtle masterfullness of Svengali   in fact I never guessed he had it in him. It is the greatest masterpiece of acting I've ever seen, speaking unpredudied it is pure and simple *genius*, it is *wonderful*   his make up is extraordainry he looks ultra devilish, when in the wretched Paris studio in his rags, in the darkness with only a blue light on his face declares he is his own god, then nearly dies and prays, and in the end in his rich cloths in the magnificent opera house with a green light on his white face with its big nose and streaming black hair, flung across a table with his head hanging down the effect is super-human!!! except perhaps for Sherlock Holmes I never enjoyed a play so much   it is the first time Trees acting has convinced me, moved and touched me, and the devilish horror of it froze me with terror, and oh! the divine applause   how I loved them   they were wonderful, how I clap-ped!! We all liked it, but I got cross with the darling Tree, at the end he waited till everyone was nearly out of the house then the curtain went up, and 'Trilby' and *he as himself in evening dress stood on the stage*!!   imagine my feelings!!!!!!!! and I was behind the barrier near the door, and had to stand on tip toe to see him at all, he was so far off I could see very little of his face (shall I put an adjective?) and that only a second, Dada hustled me off, oh I could have yelled, the *brute* why did he not come on before?!!!!

Now Olivia resumes her own story:

My recollections for the following year, 1903, are not very clear. The next letter I had from Herbert refers to a graphologist, an invalid ex-nurse in whom I was interested, and for whom I begged his name as a patron, partly I suspect to provide me with an excuse for correspondence. Nor do I know which of his plays had proved a failure, and elicited the sympathy of which he speaks. It may have been *Ulysses*, a rather dull production in which he was at his worst, as always where he was required to be martial. He was too much an artist and a dreamer to have anything in common with soldiers, who always bored him dreadfully, but his inability to represent men of action marked his one limitation in the endless gallery of types he created.

August 8   1 The Albany, London

Dear Miss Truman,

     I am sorry you are worried lest I should be angry. How could I be? Whatever you did could only have been meant kindly, and the intention is all – or nearly all – when one is young.

     I am very sensible of your kindness, and if I have not acknowledged your various letters, it is because it would not be fitting that I should encourage you to write to me. I am writing this in order that you may know I am not annoyed at anything you have done. I don't quite like the wording of the card, but then I don't like giving my name to any enterprise unless it were to do some great good.

     I am also writing to return to you some postal orders which you sent me and which I could not accept, so please do with them as you think fit.

     Some time ago you were fearful that I might worry about failure and consequent money loss – these things trouble me not at all – and I am always in high spirits during stormy times (you see, misfortune is my native element – perhaps, like Herod, I was born ' 'neath a wild moon by the sea'.) Nor am I troubled about 'honours', I rate myself far too highly for that. (Forgive this personal note.) I am very happy in your good opinion, and I hope you will always be sensible and strong-minded (in the womanly way).

     I am sure your mother won't mind my writing this – so please tell her.

Yours sincerely,
Herbert Beerbohm Tree

I rather think that after I had told my mother, as requested, of this letter, I was put on parole to desist from my correspondence, but I soon found a way to carry on as before, whilst throwing a jesuitical sop to my conscience. I left out my own name in writing to him, and signed myself 'Your Greatest Admirer' as a substitute! This silly ruse he quickly rendered useless. He had just put on *Resurrection*, and my mother herself took me to see him in it. I wrote and asked him to leave some sign at the box office for his 'Greatest Admirer'. How well I remember slinking down between the acts to find out if there was anything for me, and the bitterness of my disappointment when I learned that there was not. At the conclusion of the play we were going next door to tea at the Carlton Hotel, and when we were on our way there it struck me that the message might have come subsequently, and be waiting for me after all.

Inventing some shameless lie about having dropped something, I ran back to ask, and sure enough an envelope was handed me. I thrust it hurriedly in my dress, and rejoined my mother, but my one desire was to escape alone to see what he had sent me. Eventually the tea came to an end and we drove to Paddington for our train. Arrived there I could wait no longer, but retired to a spot guaranteed strictly private and pulled out my treasure. It was clearly marked with my name, thus ignoring the 'Greatest Admirer' pretence, and contained just his photograph signed.

Here follows Olivia's hysterical description of these events at the time. The black-edged paper was for the death of her grandmother.

22 March 1903   Stafferton Lodge, Maidenhead*

Dearest Lady,
        How incompatable this dolorous edge is with the wild mad joy at my heart! Never, never have I been so wild about seeing him before, I suppose because it was put off once, and all this week I have been ill, yes really ill with excitement I could not eat. I felt so sick, was always trembling and was besieged with fears it might go wrong again, anyhow it was with difficulty I restrained a collapse. (I can hear you say 'little ass'. But Miss Mackay once you were my age, you must know, you must understand!) . . . Ultimately I went to tea at Stella's [Stella Buchanan was a close friend of Olivia's] . . . Well there I met a young man (her cousin) who is thinking of going on the stage, and seems very much in the 'know' about H going to rehearsals there ect: Four years ago at the dress rehearsal of 'King John' (the youth was present) . . . H finished a magnificent tableau. About 50 of his friends were there. He asked one 'What do you think of it?' 'It might be improved' was the answer. Then H turned to his wife 'Well, my dear and what do *you* think of it?' 'I agree with Mr So-and-so' she answered . . . that wicked woman wounded his very soul, weary as it was – he cried on the stage! I had much ado to keep from doing so too when this was told me. ah! my dear this is one scene of many, poor heart, poor heart, after 19 years she has not taken the trouble to understand him, but I know all it means to him, I went back, my mind full of pain and longing for him, it haunted me all night. The next day I wrote to him unsigned, unaddressed, I asked him if moments never came when after all his dreaming and toiling others, to show their knowledge tho'

* On her father's retirement he sold the house in Taplow (where they had lived for four years) and the family now rented a succession of houses in Maidenhead and Bray while looking for a suitable permanent residence.

they could not excel what he had created, because they were jealous disparaged it, did he never ask then does *no one* understand? I told him I was coming to him on Saturday   that I at least in that vast audience knew what it meant to him, I asked him if the knowledge that at moments when he felt that no one else on earth understood, that I did, was any help to him, to send an unaddressed note to the Box Office where I could call for it after the performance, that he was only to send it if from his heart he found that I who knew all it meant to him, was a real help to him being in the audience. Miss Mackay he sent it!!! You have no idea all it means to me, it is no silly craving for a love letter, it means that I, I, I insignificant little me, really am some use to that great man, that I help the one I adore, a thing I thought impossible, indeed dreamed the reverse. And that is not all it means, he addressed it to 'Miss Truman'   guessed whom his letter was from tho' my writing is quite different from when I first wrote him 'billet-doux'! . . . It was the proof of a photograph of himself as the handsome dashing soldier making love to Lena Ashwell as the young innocent girl, he is about to kiss her – it was signed by himself. That was all there was no other word: it was enough, don't you see what it means, why he should have chosen that particular picture? because, because he places me in the young girls place, she is a type of me, – it means, it means he would kiss me!!!!!!!!!! his forgiveness for the old wrong, his gratitude for my present understanding, his kiss for the future!!! The one thing I have hoped and longed and prayed for, of which he has given no indication before has come to pass! You will ask what colour my cheeks are when I say the realization of that kiss is all I ask better, and now perhaps some day it may! are you surprised I am crazy with joy? I send you a critic on the play   it was very difficult to do, it is quite true they don't believe what they say, and he doesn't, I know when he doesn't because he strikes attitudes at once, but I was very deeply touched when he said and meant it 'Love is everything'. 'The only true happiness in life is to live for others'   he looked very handsome, and played with an air of quiet, powerful distinction that was extraordainery. I have never seen him make every day love before, he was EXQUISITE so natural and such a gentleman, I nearly died of jealousy, he did it so well, raining kisses on her, mine was *real* jealousy, not like Mrs Trees afraid he may not pay enough attention to her in public and so hurt her pride, not because she cares about him, *I* envied every embrace . . .

Your,
Olivia

P.S. Please return critic.
P.P.S. Of course you will regard all this in strictest confidence, but I had

to let it out or I should have been ill, the suppression of the last week has been awful.

In the next letter I received from him (dated April 28th, 1903) appears a new and more intimate note. My persistence, and the depth of my devotion, were beginning to have their effect on him:

My dear Miss Truman,

       I hardly know how to write to you. I do deeply appreciate the kind and beautiful letter you wrote to me, and I am very proud to think that I should have been the means of inspiring such sweet and noble thoughts in you. I have not written because I did not think it right to enter into a correspondence with you, and so encourage a feeling which is only a passing phase and which I hope will in time give place to a great-hearted devotion to someone who is worthy of it. I only wish to assure you that I am not indifferent to your kindness, for I should indeed be ungrateful if I did not appreciate it.

       I would most gladly see you if your mother were with you. I will send the picture for which you asked me.

       I have been much worried and preoccupied of late. I am delighted to think that 'Resurrection' has appealed to you in the same way that it appealed to me – it has been a rare joy to give it to the people.

       With all my heart's best wishes,

I am, Yours sincerely,
Herbert Beerbohm Tree

I must have thought that the moment was ripe for a further step, for evidently I was trying to see him. I do not know the occasion of the following undated notes, both sent from His Majesty's Theatre, but as I certainly did *not* meet him, I conclude that my mother had not been included in my schemes and could not be produced.

Many, many thanks for your kind thought and congratulations. I would prefer to wait till your mother comes. In haste,

Yours sincerely,
H.B.T.

With pleasure – if your mother is with you – will you see me? H.B.T.

I then tried a flank attack. My time being not as much occupied with my education as it should have been, when I was not concocting some ridiculous novel or other under the influence of Hall Caine or Marie Corelli, I had taken to writing to any celebrity who caught my fancy. Nobody was quite safe from me, and strange as it may seem I had the gift of making my victims reply to my unsolicited outpourings. Now I thought I would try my hand with Herbert's half-brother, the great Max Beerbohm. I must have desired to send my beloved some Easter greeting in keeping with the play *Resurrection*, and not knowing where he would be for the holiday, made this an excuse to write to Max, from whom I received the following crushing answer:

7 April 1903   48 Upper Berkeley Street, W.

Dear Madam,

   I do not know where my brother is going to spend Easter; and really you must excuse me for not trying to discover the place and informing you of it.

   You see, I have not the pleasure of knowing you (a pleasure to come, some day, I hope). Nor do you tell me what is your motive (or your anxiety). In this ill-regulated world one has to be careful; and for all I know, you may be an anarchist, eager to throw a bomb (skilfully disguised as an Easter egg) at my brother, as being a representative of 'things as they are'.

   Probably you are not an anarchist at all. But you certainly are mysterious, and must, I repeat, excuse me.

Faithfully yours,
Max Beerbohm

P.S. You may, of course, rely absolutely on me not to show your letter to anyone.

Characteristically I remained undaunted, and succeeded in eliciting these four delightful letters:

Thursday   48 Upper Berkeley Street, W.

Dear Miss Truman,

   Please don't speak of any 'sacrifice of modesty'. There is nothing for you to be ashamed of. Yours seems to me a very natural little case. I myself, at your age, cherished a remote passion for an actress. And I remember that she too, in answer to one of my epistles, said that my insight into her character was 'a great help' to her. All young gentlemen and most young ladies pass through this kind of phase, and the objects of their adoration always profess to be greatly helped by it. 'Profess' is not quite a just word, perhaps. They really are helped. It ministers to that particular kind of vanity which, whether they be men or women, the life of the stage fosters in them. I wish I were still young enough to help them thus. But my age is, alas! just about half-way between yours and my brother's. I can only contemplate these idylls from without. To be dragged into one of them as a go-between, I must respectfully decline. I am very sorry indeed to refuse your request. But my sense of humour and honour and so forth prevents me. So here are the beautiful photograph and the beautiful letter and the sealed telegram which is, I am sure, as beautiful as they. And I am, with many regrets,

Max Beerbohm

19 April 1903   Savile Club, 107 Piccadilly, W.

Dear Miss Truman,

Your last letter (which I should have answered days ago, only I have been away and had none of my letters forwarded to me) is (excuse that long parenthesis) full of fallacies.

1. I am not at all Scotch. That quality of caution which you contemn in me is due to an admixture of Dutch blood. (Beerboom is the original version of my name. Holland is a delightful little nation in its way, with a fine past; and I am sure you will be glad to know that my brother originates from it.)

2. I am always quite serious. Your notion of me as a compound of frivolity and caution is manifestly absurd.

3. I am not married.

Having ventured to correct these details about myself, let me now withdraw unreservedly my hint that yours was 'a very usual little case'. This I said merely to comfort you. I was conscious of having stumbled on a tremendous and soul-stirring tragedy. There never has been anything like it. I search the world's history in vain for any analogue to you or to my brother. I wish I were a poet and could hand you both down to posterity.

A mere prosaist, I find great pleasure in the prospect of meeting you both at tea. Please don't forget your promise to arrange that meeting, and believe me,

Yours very truly,
Max Beerbohm

21 April 1903   48 Upper Berkeley Street, W.

Dear Miss Truman,

I look forward to the postponed pleasure. But I am afraid the postponement may mean that the pleasure never will come off. 'Going abroad' usually means staying in Paris on the way. I foresee you hopelessly in love with Coquelin *aîné*, and writing earnestly to Coquelin *cadet* to ascertain where his brother means to spend Whitsuntide, also to implore *cadet* to nip in the bud the dreadful stories circulated about *aîné*'s private life. I am very sorry that people are (apparently) talking scandal to you about my brother. But I don't think it really matters very much. Scandal always is talked about anyone worth talking about. If one happens to like the public person in question, one need only lay one's hand on one's heart and say that one's interlocutor is misinformed. This, at least, is what I always do. And in the case of my brother, I should be able to do it without violence to my conscience. Indeed, you are the nearest approach to anything scandalous known by me about him authentically. And this scandal consists merely in his having said that he finds your sympathy 'a great help' to him – bless him!

I *don't* 'hate' you, and you *are* 'delightful'. Excuse my negligence in not having till now paid you the compliments for which you had been so very patiently fishing. And believe me that the compliment is not the less sincere because you have (as who should say) used a landing-net.

To the possible pleasure of our meeting,

Yours very truly,
Max Beerbohm

By 'possible' I don't imply a doubt of the pleasure, on my side. Merely a doubt of the meeting itself. Coquelin is very overwhelming.

                                       Hartley Grange, Winchfield, Hants
Sunday

Dear Miss Truman,

No, indeed I had not forgotten – but I had supposed you had by this time. Your fidelity to the ideal of my brother is very surprising and beautiful and touching. Alas, I shall not have even that modified meeting which you offer me for tomorrow night. I have promised to stay here for several days and cannot break my promise. I hope very much that the stars in their courses will bring us face to face before long, and that you will be duly dazzled by my reflected glory. You certainly have the power of exciting one's curiosity; you hint that you are 'femine'. Femineness must be a delightful quality – I shall not rest till I have beheld an example of it. Also, it seems, you are 'unconspicous'. That again is very rare. Finally you give me permission to call you a 'prigg'. What, oh what, is a prigg? It is quite awful to think that in stall sixteen of the upper circle will be sitting tomorrow night an unconspicous femine prigg and that I shall not be there to see. Beside me on this writing table is a crystal – if only I were a clairvoyant!

I hope you will have a very nice evening. My brother has a very good part in the Kipling affair, he dies on the stage and is covered with the Union Jack. Do not drown the stalls with your tears; buckets can be obtained from the attendants.

I am, my dear Miss Truman,   Yours very truly,
Max Beerbohm

I am flattered by your suggestion that I should write my memoirs, only my life has been so very uneventful; the nearest approach to luridness was that I almost met you, and it would hardly fill a volume to say 'It was about this time that I almost met that remarkable woman Olivia Truman. Beautiful, in the strict sense of the word, she was not, but she had the remains of great prettiness, and was liable to become pretty again at any moment. She had, moreover, her 'nice nights', one of which was the one on which I did not meet her. She is said to have been the one and only authentic prigg the world has ever known, and there is little doubt that she was conspicously femine. To have almost met her is to have lived not in vain.'

The 'Kipling affair' mentioned by Max was The Man Who Was, *and his warning to Olivia not to drown the stalls with her tears accurately forecast her reaction given in the following letter, written just as her family was in the middle of moving.*

10 June 1903   Stafferton Lodge, Maidenhead

Dearest Lady,

I am snatching a moment with practically one foot in the street t'other in doors we are reduced to a few beds a table and two chairs! I have no time to speak as much as I should like of Monday, only the house was brilliant, besides King, Queen, Princess Victoria, Princess of Wales, I was *so* proud! The orchestra usually covered in palm leaves was one blazing mass of red and pink roses that smelt – !!!! 'Flodden Field' was without exception the most boring piece ever staged I could barely sit thro' it, or keep awake, ME, at *His Majesty's*!! It was however *beautifully* staged and well acted 'The Man Who Was' is without exception the most wonderful thing ever done on the modern stage, you would not believe that such acting as H's possible   Even I, much as I love him and know his every small action could find no trace of Beerbohm Tree in the little shrivelled long haired, white bearded, monkey like monster, clothed in nothing but a few rags. He was supposed to have escaped from Siberia after twenty years to his old regiment, to have forgotten himself and speech, to see him running about feeling things, muttering like a baby was *too* too dreadful, it made me quite ill and when he sat and sobbed my God! may I never hear such a sound again, I closed my ears it was too painful. He resembled Rip van Winkle more than anything only more so, and before I was utterly overcome I had time to admire his legs which were *quite* bare and *beautifully* moulded! He held the house in vice of iron by the sheer force and tragedy of his play, we were so strung up we could not even weep and scarcely breathe, and by the end we were almost stunned by the blinding emotions he conjured up. It was almost too terrific and it was entirely him   Beyond all doubt now he is the greatest actor of the century!! How proud I am of him, how daring I feel to love him! at the end I shook myself free from his deadly spell and *shouted* clear above others 'Tree, Tree, Tree'   I clapped I stamped, I cheered, how glad I was to be in the Upper Circle so I could! . . .

Your ever,
Olivia

There follows a description of Tree's Richard II *which, even from a besotted fifteen-year-old, is not without interest.*

18 September 1903   Fernley, Maidenhead

My dearest Lady,

I am safely back as you see   On Monday I said good-bye at the Rocks and in the afternoon tried to make sweets, we made a huge mess and no sweets eatable and felt very happy! I was so disappointed   Mother was to have met me and taken me to 'Richard II' but wired me on Tuesday night she did not feel up to it so I went with Bobby [her old nurse, 'Bobby' Lee]. My dear, it is so wonderful! You will see all about it in the enclosed critique which I call quite the best thing I have ever written. But there is one thing that I have not put down and which none of that vast assembly (the house was '*full*') will ever know, he looked at me, he thought of me, and as God lives he played to me, and me alone!!! I know it I cannot tell how only I am quite *quite* sure and never has he acted better, or have I felt so proud!! There was a point in that play where I was *mad* for love of him, I refere to it in my critique, I mean the Westminster Hall scene. Picture him. The old hall with the brilliant scarlet and black robed throng of priests and peers, the high, gold canopyed throne, himself sitting in a pure-white brocade underdress, quite straight and plain down to the feet, a huge violet velvet mantle bordered in gold and lined with ermine, the great gold sceptre, the flashing diadem, and the lights through the stained glass falling on the fair hair and blue eyes. Every inch he was a king, and I doubt whether Richard ever poised his head with such regal grace, or made his fellow men look so poor! Again I have never seen anything more pathetic than when stripped of his regalia, in his unadorned white robe, he first seeks his friends in the room to bid good-bye to, and finds but two, and then alone, and almost a prisoner leaves the hall, and yet at that minute Bolingbroke on the throne did not look as imperial as the tall fair haired, white gowned unattended monarch, oh! it was magnificent! . . .

On December 13th, 1903 Olivia described a visit to London with her mother:

. . . We 'teaed' at the Carlton, and I saw – H! He came with Constance Collier (looking wonderful) at whom he gazed as if he could eat her – with rapture! He neither bowed nor spoke to me, tho' he looked at me often and I'm sure knew me, he only stayed a little, and they went without tea, which looked very mad. He was looking well, and taller than ever. Do you know I was not the least excited or even pleased, only vastly irritated he didn't come and speak! It was to-day 2 years ago I saw him last, it has been a long time to wait for such a little glimpse, when you know the secret of those two years you will know in them he has turned me – my nature – into a womans. Mrs Adams [presumably a friend of her mother's] complained I was too grown up, it was not likely I should remain a baby, when the noblest side of a more passionate love than she ever felt, was daily mastering me . . .

On January 24th, 1904 she records her impressions of The Darling of the Gods:

. . . The play as one had always been led to suppose – well you will see my opinion in the enclosed criticism, though so beautiful is the production I dare not even *attempt* to describe it! What my beloved looked like you cannot think!! Imagine a man with his hair arranged so: behind and bald except for one long curl in front, a man with a yellow parchment face, and flabby double chin, a man with the wickedest mouth, and most evil expression, slouching along on noiseless feet, with bent back, and under an inverted tray tied on with ear flaps, grinning cruelly, then perhaps you will have a faint idea of the man I worship! When I tell you he was never Tree, for when he spoke even it was as if Tree's voice had somehow fled to someone else, you will understand how perfect was the make-up, the whole evening I never once saw the famous eyes! His part was very small really, and so subordinate I think there was only one person there present who kept her eyes fixed on the figure of the genius who had brought it all into being! I cannot speak enough of the finish of detail and etiquette all through the wealth of soul and imagination in it, all of which I need not say was entirely lost on a stolid British audience. Good heavens they hadn't even the decency to call him at the end! I could have killed them I was dying to see him so   Vapid brutes, in the last scene in Heaven a woman behind me said 'Have you been playing much bridge lately?' My dear, I could have struck the creature dead! It makes me so sick to think that H has to dance about for the amusement of a crew of fools who don't understand art and aren't fit to wash his area steps for him! Of course he was very wonderful in it, but I liked him better in 'Richard' and as to me his part makes the play, you can guess which I liked best, one is the genius of the actor, the other the artist – I prefere having my heart charmed to my eye . . .

At this time for some obscure reason she had yielded to the advice of her current governess that her passion for Tree was wrong, and had attempted to cut him out of her life, only succeeding in making herself very miserable in the process, as many introspective letters to Miss Mackay bear witness. However she seems to have cheered herself up a bit with the thought of Max:

. . . But ah! my dear how sad I felt! This time last year how happy I was in the first sunshine of his goodness, it was the first opening of that real passion of love that the year unfolded   'Resurrection' oh! yes – and the telegram!! By-the-bye also it is exactly a year since Max and I flashed wit on wit, for since I had sounded him I flatter myself brilliant creature as he is I was no second to him – if I was not he would never have troubled with me! Mon dieu I have never laughed so much since!! Well, well I have done with one brother, thank goodness not being in love with the other I may hope for a deal more fun out of him when I'm out and go to town! Yes I believe I have a fairly unique record when I reflect that 4 celebrated men told me – me an infant of 15! that I was delightful in a year . . .

Olivia's narrative resumes: There is a long space before I contrived to wring another answer out of Herbert, but that I had not abandoned hope, nor he receded from his position, is evident from the following:

3 August 1904   Gruenes Kreuz, Marienbad

Dear Miss Truman,

You will, I hope, have not misunderstood my motives in not writing to thank you for the many kind letters you have written to me, but believe me, I deeply appreciate the interest you have been good enough to take in me and my affairs. I am indeed grateful to you for much encouragement and I am proud of your good opinion.

You prettily suggested that I should send you some trifling remembrance that you could keep. I am sending you a very simple little keepsake, on which you will perhaps have your seal engraved.

All has gone well this year, and now that you are growing up, I hope you are very happy.

Believe me, with renewed thanks for your kindness,

Yours sincerely,
Herbert Beerbohm Tree

I was much touched by what you wrote me as to the influence that I had been in your life. H.B.T.

During this time we had changed our residence several times. With my father's retirement from the War Office there was no longer any necessity to live near London, and my parents eventually found a place to suit them between Lymington and Milford-on-Sea* – a 'mansion' requiring eight servants apart from Mother's lady's maid, with fifteen acres of garden, about five gardeners, two laundrymaids for its private laundry, and a coachman and grooms.

I was still wasting a lot of paper in writing romances. The shilling shockers had given way to stories much influenced by Marie Corelli and Hall Caine. My mother was a great reader, and got me to read aloud to her for hours daily – it was about the only education I had – but she confined her subjects to memoirs and novels. She was very ambitious for me, but as I have said, never gave me a proper education, and though herself a woman of the world, having mixed with distinguished and intelligent people, she permitted me to indulge

* The place that suited them was Efford Park which was to be Olivia's home for the next two years.

21

in the silliest whims, and in my ignorance to damn myself socially. My father, had he lived, might have done something to stop this, but he died when I was just seventeen. He had been in poor health ever since he had an epileptic stroke brought on by the Remount Enquiry after the Boer War, and eventually developed Bright's Disease. I felt hardly any reaction to his passing: we had never had anything in common and I think he was jealous of my mother's affection for me. At the end he had four nurses, and numerous cylinders of oxygen to keep him alive an extra six weeks of misery. Then we all trailed behind his motor hearse to Woking where a regimental guard awaited us, and after the short ceremony we returned wearily to Efford.* One vital change his death made in my life: the last obstacle was removed from my personal approach to Tree.

The 'period of renunciation' was happily over after Herbert's letter of August 3rd, and Olivia was taken to see Tree's new production of The Tempest *in which he himself played Caliban, Viola his daughter played Ariel, and Lionel Brough, Stephano. On October 8th she wrote to Miss Mackay:*

. . . very oddly Madame had a box that night so that wife and daughter were before me! Viola – the dear girl is lovely and *so* graceful! It is such a wonderfully mobile face, and rightly they speak of the beauty of her voice!! The part tho' is one little fitted to her – quite correctly in doing a spirit – a thing of air, she flits here and there, swaying about everywhere – with a woman of her stature it merely strikes one as restlessness which fidgets – she too, wears short skirts which don't suit her a bit, but she shows every sign of great powers and by her extraordainery flow of life and spirits triumphs even now! What my lord looked like is impossible to describe – suffice it he is covered in long cocanut hairs, and wig all over his shoulders which are dyed blue, long nails, tusks, and crawls mostly on the ground! He even *licks* the soles of Brough's feet! – how can he? – and why does he? Beyond this the play is wonderful, but contrary to what the critics say I do not see he surpasses all former creation – it does not for instance touche the poetic spirit of 'Ulysses' However it is undoubtidly charming. Mother was so bored she nearly yawned her inside out – but then she is neither a Shakespearian student, nor a lover of the drama . . . My feelings were very mixed there, he, with his wife and child was somthing new – I felt peculilarly that altho' he fills all my life, I have no place in his, and I

---

* The reader should perhaps be warned that Olivia's father has not in fact made his last appearance. There are several references to him in letters to Miss Mackay which observe (as Olivia's narrative does not) strict chronological order.

envied those who do – the child has so much of his mirth in her – yet someday – that far day – perhaps it will be the other way on! – When he came before the curtain he straightened his humped back and shoulder, and drew himself up – beast as his make up made him he carried himself with the loftiness and dignity of a king – is it not ever so, don deformity in mind or body how he will, the greatness of both leeks out . . .

It is interesting that just at this point, and abandoning the 't's which she had for some time been copying from the actor William Gillette, her writing became perfectly formed and took on the character it was to retain for the rest of her life. She was sixteen and a half.

1905

In May 1905 Olivia and both her parents saw Business is Business in which Tree scored a notable success, though as a result of whatever pressures the play, showing a Jewish businessman in an unflattering light, was soon taken off. She often referred to her father as 'the General' in letters to Miss Mackay.

May 18   Efford Park, Lymington, Hants

Dearest Aunt Judy,*
      I am bursting – positively *bursting* with joy!! – was there ever such a triumph – and such a man!!! – the criticisms are somthing dazzling – it seems to be the creation of his life – and at his age!! what vitality! – and what think you – Mother went to see it with the General on Wednesday!! – I made her – a discreet remark on what a wonderful thing it seemed to be in my letter to her – she says that she has been to many plays for many years – and she has *never* seen anything to approach it – that it is incredible – a marvel – a performance that would even question the world-wide supremacy of Coquelin!!!!! all this she told me – and I listened giddy with pride! Even the General is astounded and you know how he dislikes Herbert! and yet I do not think it will come as such a revelation to me as to them – I saw 'The Man Who Was' – they did not – and after that extraordinary display of genius I can believe anything of him! How I waited and feared Saturday and Sunday! The latter was a torment of anxiety – all the critical hour of 9 to 10 to the former I was on my knees praying for his inspiration and his courage – but I never dared to hope that God would answer my prayer so gorgeously – I have the vanity to imagine that perhaps my pleading helped a little!! – in the glory of such a triumph my own puny affairs are swallowed up – and yet – that man *shall* be mine! . . .

* This was the name Olivia now settled on for Miss Mackay.

25

Then, about ten days later, she attained the goal of her ambition. She was in another theatre, watching a comedy:

. . . I stood it for five minutes – then got up, walked out and into His Majesty's!!!!!!! I asked for seats and got them, having no money said I would send it – not intending to – and took possession. A crumpled old envelope picked up off the floor – a pencil borrowed from an attendant – and Mr H. Beerbohm Tree was made acquainted with both my finances and my whereabouts (the note was open:) The result was a divine scrawl in reply (also open) presenting me with the places, a lovely signed souvenir of himself in all his Shakespeare week roles – and a request that if Mother were with me I would see him. [Two lines of exclamation marks.]

The eyes of my neighbours nearly dropped out of their heads with awe at my corresponding with the actor manager. I grew inches taller and replied 'No answer'!!! It is not vanity on my part that causes me to say that in the next two acts he paid more attention to me than his part, and it was to me that he looked for applause (which he got!) I returned home speechless with emotion and spent hours composing a letter to him which ultimately resolved itself into a few words thanking him for the seats and the souvenir, and saying I refused to see him because I loved him – what else or what less could I? But he must be a blooming fool to think I could ever meet him   however he too suffers from the passing phase idea and seems to imagine every 6 weeks that it has passed!! but the position has altered   at last he sues and I refuse. Have I done wrong? Tell me that – I do not know – I put myself in the way of a very great temptation. I resisted it because I was in the mood to – if I hadn't been – what then?

Then, in July, came the first night of Oliver Twist:

Dearest Aunt Judy,

Que Dieu est bon! Je lui remercie de toute mon ame!! and then too I can never be grateful enough for having had the privilege to be present at the first night!! To speak consecutively (which is difficult in this heat!!) instead of the play being the uninteresting failure I had not the slightest doubt it would be – that extraordinary playwright Comyns Carr has worked the book not only into a good play but a great success. I do not know exactly what the papers say about it – but I gather they are unfavourable – it is inexplicable for the applause were perfectly boundless – the house regularly went mad over it – and I with it! Le bon Dieu sait my arms are stiff and swollen now – not merely from joining in the clapping but from leading the gallery to the charge again and again   and to crown all when Herbert came forward to make a really pretty and heartfelt speech – rendered all the more telling by so excessive a nervousness that he could say nothing but the same thing over and over again . . .

Well to crown my evenings performance I jumped up on my stall. I question whether such a thing has ever been done by a woman in West End stalls before. However for that I cared nothing and my face far back as it was must have stood out to him above all others. Thank goodness M. Jean had dressed my hair and that it was generally thought I had never looked so well before. It was also a great happiness to me that before such a triumph I sent him a scrap of white heather in one of his own ticket envelopes – so that he could not have known it was I – unless he guessed which is probable. But that wasn't wrong was it? . . . Among a very smart audience I recognised Joe Chamberlain, Lady Colin Campbell, Bancroft, Lily Hanbury, Laurence Irving, Mrs and Miss Tree – the former of the last two behaved like a swine though she looked beautiful as she never once went round to congratulate Herbert – she was *too* funny over Constance Collier   going white and red as she came before the curtain. I expect I was as bad – Herbert should have felt very complacent in the middle of 3 women all *wildly* in love with him!! As a matter of fact – the other two I should think make a hell for him!! Some instinct tells me for certain that Constance Collier is his mistress! And so the season ended with eclat.

The next of Olivia's letters refers to the cracking of the proscenium arch at His Majesty's under the weight of the steel safety curtain.

September 27   Efford Park, Lymington

My dearest Aunt Judy,

Anxious as I am to know how you are getting on and to cheer you up, I must confess everything save Herbert has been put out of my head by this *appalling* accident at His Majesty's!! – I learnt of it from Miss Weldon when I went to my singing lesson yesterday morning and nearly went into hysterics! – dear heaven what he will lose! – not only will the repairs be somthing frightful – but besides the hire of the Waldorf and his own current expenses – he must pay the retaining fees of those actors who were to have appeared at the latter theatre – I suppose a prolonged run of such a giant success as 'Oliver Twist' will be the only means of recouping a bit – but one never knows if he will consent to be sensible enough to do it – and then this insane scheme of his to put Viola in the title role of 'Joan of Arc' to be done with unheard of magnificence – it would have been ridiculous to have expected Bernhardt herself to have sustained the leading role at the leading theatre, with only 18 months experience behind her – and certainly Viola is not la divine Sarah! – if that is a failure on top of this, I only see one thing before him – and yet – did he not pull thro' when he had just built His Majesty's and crowned it with a fiasco of a piece? – Such courage, such resource as he has wants some beating – could anything be more marvellous than the way he seized on the Waldorf at 11 at night and spent all the silent hours when London slept tearing between the two buildings superintending the moving operations? – I think he may share Bismarck's title of the 'man of iron' – and yet at such a moment within twenty minutes of the time that he has to appear at a theatre a mile away – he finds leisure to remember a person he has scarcely seen – and telegraph to her!!!!!!!!!!!!

Yes – it is absolutely a fact – of course as was inevitable I wrote him a note there and then on hearing the news – I don't quite know what I said, but sufficient at least to make it extremely humourous that it should be written with the pencil of such an exceedingly correct person as Miss Weldon – a pencil that very likely had never done anything but mark mistakes in correct young ladies incorrect singing – a pencil, that if it could have understood that it was conveying a good many 'darlings' to a married man, would very likely have refused to mark!! – but the result that pencil brought about was inconceivable – picture me playing with food that my continued perturbation of mind made impossible for me to eat – but looking immaculately proper in my well ordered surroundings – see Sunny Jim strut in with a telegram and hand it to a me, the color of a tomato – see me peruse the astounding message 'Thousand thanks for your sympathy – all is well – am writing' and realize with such a flood of emotion as had never been mine before, that in that crisis I was present to him – then see me with a hand that did not even faintly tremble put the wire in my lap, and looking quietly up inform my inquiring parents that the Wade girl regretted being unable to come to tea to-morrow!!!!!!

On October 9th Herbert wrote from the Garrick Club:

My dear Miss Truman,
    I have great pleasure in sending you the voucher for Thursday next. It will be a great pleasure to know you are present.
    And how can I thank you for your delightful little gift which I shall always prize among my most sacred possessions?
    I had intended writing to you in reply to your letters, but I daresay you

will understand how difficult it is for me to do so. I have many duties in my life of which you do not know, but it has always been a dear encouragement to me to know that there was one who gave me such kind thoughts; and I have felt proud to know that I have through my work been able to exercise a good and lasting influence.

By the bye, since you sing, pray get a beautiful little song called 'A Child's Prayer', the last lines of which are about a song 'that helpeth others to be strong and makes the singer glad'. I think I like it better than any song I know, but it is (unlike me) very young and simple.

Your mother has kindly written to me – if she is there, perhaps I may see you on Thursday?

Yours sincerely,
Herbert Beerbohm Tree

And again on October 16th:

My dear Miss Truman,

Many thanks for your kind letter. I cannot express to you how grateful I am for your goodness to me, but I should ill repay that goodness by asking you to see me.

Of course I regarded you as a child hitherto, but I realise that you have grown to womanhood. It *would not be right* – there is no other reason – that we should meet. Please, please, think of me only as one who deeply appreciates your goodness, you would only spoil your life if I were to intrude into it. It would be a great pleasure to me if you would write to me, but I have been thinking a great deal about you and I know I am right.

You will marry somebody who will make you happy, I hope, but do be very sane and remember that you are the most important thing on earth to yourself.

I should like to send you a book of Joan of Arc – may I?

I should much like to see your mother with you – but I suppose it would seem odd.

Thank you again – I understand – and so do you, I hope.

Yours sincerely,
H.B.T.

P.S. I have been terribly busy and worried about the death of Irving – for me the position was peculiarly difficult.

Yet some time between then and the death of my father on November 9th we met. By what means I broke down his resistance, I do not know, probably by some ruse or other. Anyhow there came a moment when I found myself in the lift which ascended to the dome of His Majesty's where he had made his private apartments. High up they were, and to me as high as heaven, which would have seemed a comparatively unimportant place. I had garbed myself for the occasion in a sort of bridal array which in retrospect seems almost past belief. I wore a coat and skirt of eighteenth-century design in fawn cloth, a flowing skirt, and tight-fitting three-quarter coat with revers and cuffs of pink and blue brocade, lace ruffles and paste buttons! On top of my hair, done over a Pompadour roll in the style of the moment, I had a blue straw hat, tipped forward, and piled up at the back with pink roses. I fancied myself tremendously in this amazing rig-out.

Of what followed I have but a blurred recollection. My head was awhirl with the strength of my emotion. I know how wonderful it seemed when he led me down the little winding passage, and through the huge nail-studded doors into the big banqueting hall, with its long tables, and its frieze of paintings of his plays, and then through the heavy curtains screening off his own sanctum. Every detail that I got to know so well rises before me: the carved centre table used for his intimate suppers, the roll-top desk bearing his father's photo, the armchair, now in my possession, green-covered like the floor and the settee beneath the bookcases; the open fire. On the walls were more paintings of Shakespearean subjects, with the windows set high up, letting in the rumble of the traffic far below. Ah, the marvellous atmosphere of that room which had caught so much of his personality. Even when I went back to it recently, and all his furnishings had vanished, and instead the prosaic arrangements for committee meetings had been substituted – it was still there, terrible in its actuality for one who had loved him. No wonder they say he haunts the dome, but it is no ghostly apparition, just the ineffaceable impress of his master mind.

So there at last, remote above the roofs of London, we faced each other alone. I don't know what we said. I expect we were both a little shy, but gallantry at least demanded one thing, and Herbert, bless him, was always gallant. Strange that there is but one manner of expressing the hired passion of the harlot, and the love which is eternal. Kisses to Herbert must have meant but little, they do not mean much to any man, but to me the contact of his lips was more holy than any sacrament. Everything I had to offer of body, soul and spirit, I gave him then. That I never became his mistress in the accepted sense of the word is true, and there are people who seem to think that such a thing is of importance, marking the line between what is 'moral' and what is 'immoral', as if a mere physical act, taken by itself, can have any significance other than legal. A thousand nights of mere passion will not bring two beings any nearer to each other. Nothing except the outpouring of the inner being can do that. I belonged to Herbert absolutely and utterly. Had I lived with him always, I could have added nothing more; that is why I know that death cannot, and has not parted us.

This is how Olivia described the occasion to Miss Mackay at the time:

24 October 1905

. . . I looked very well that night and my hair was perfectly done. You know he gave us the royal box where Maude [Herbert's wife, Maud Tree] generally is and put her down below! Herbert sent for me in the second act and Lady Emily [Lady Emily Alexander, the mother of Olivia's old playmates] came too – he looked awful as Fagin close by – all in stripes of green and red – he was dreadfully gauche and jumpy and it wanted all my savoir faire to carry it thro' – he showed us the rooms in the Dome which I have always wanted to see so much – they are quite exquisite – we did not stay very long. I managed by pretending to lose my bracelet to get back to him for a second later, and he gave me an appointment for the next day. The Alexanders all enjoyed the play hugely – tho' Herbert was not up to the mark – I was the only person in the house he looked at! I met him at the theatre next day, and after a little talk in his room – drove down to the city with him and then about London for nearly an hour! It was all very astonishing – I had always thought that if he *did* see me – he would adopt the bon papa attitude – I think laying one's head on a lady's shoulder hardly suggests that – what do you think?!! He made love quite beautifully and just like a boy. I have nowhere seen such amazing vitality. He is a simple mass of inconsistancy and so wayward – that it is I who guide him and not he me – he and his happiness have been given into my hands – a terrible responsibility – we arrived at a very good understanding tho'   I am to be an old maid – unless he dies – for one thing I wanted to know what he would do if I married and then lost my head and came to him and he said he didn't know – that being the case all thoughts on matrimony must be at an end – I kicked against it frightfully at first. I have been so inordinately ambitious, but I soon got over that – and am now fully resigned to thick boots and good works! He told me that I was much prettier and much more fascinating than he thought. I believe that if he were free he would marry me like a shot – well, who knows – so ended our meeting – tho' he behaved so unexpectidly it came as no shock to me, and there seemed an intimacy as of many years companionship. He told me anything and everything unreservidly and in many ways he is a far better man than I thought – for one thing he has never deliberately seduced a woman – for another he has never touched his wife. [It is not clear what Olivia can have meant by this.] He is quite different from all his pictures, much younger and gentler looking, and his skin instead of being yellow and freckled as I had always fancied is fine and fresh – and I am in a position to judge!!! Some things are wierd – all this happened on Friday 13th, it was on Friday Dec 13th four years ago that I met him last – I dreamed once that he took me in his arms and kissed me – on the roof of his house – and it was high above the chimney pots of London that our lips met – I dreamed that I asked him to turn to the light so that I might look into his eyes – and so it was!! Of course the night that followed was horrible   for hours it was touche and go – but I won thro' it – and the next few days. I was with him again for over an hour on Wednesday with Evelyn [Olivia's close friend, Evelyn Alexander]. I think it was more wonderful than the other interview – there seemed to be no time we had not been together – no time we should not be together – there was no stress of emotion and no passion – we talked as the thoughts came into our heads – the grave thro' the gay – the misery thro' the happiness – and he ate his lunch while we were there – it was an absolute harmony – a chapter out of heaven – that hour – and he felt it – he told me he felt as if he had been everything to me – so perfect was the understanding – there was even no awkwardness about him – and he marvelled how he could stand with my arms round his neck and not feel ashamed and yet he did – such an experience had never been his before – strange my nature asked for no more. Instead of desire his touche brought me peace and content – not so him – such passion was in him that if he had been alone – and yet he loves another! – but I am sure now I would have made him happy and I think he thinks so too   and such neglect – and such untidiness! His writing table and a huge pile of unsorted and unanswered letters . . .

Within a few weeks of our meeting my father died, and I received this letter from Herbert – how curious that he should still have addressed me so ceremoniously!

7 November 1905   His Majesty's Theatre

My dear Miss Truman,
    I have written a few lines to your mother, but don't give them to her if it would only render her sadder.

I am thinking of you and her today. I understand all you have said to me. Perhaps one day your mother will bring you to London. Please let me know if I can do anything for you. I wish you every blessing. Thank you for all your goodness and help,

Your always sincerely,
H.B.T.

❁

I think it must have been within the next month or two that I drove with him to Putney. I know it was winter, and that I was in mourning. I think I met him at the theatre and that he called on Sir George Lewis [the eminent divorce lawyer] in the Temple, leaving me outside, but subsequently I so often drove with him, and was so often left outside, that I cannot say for certain. Anyhow we *did* go in a four-wheeler all the way to Putney which reminds me that I have made no mention of how in the early days of my infatuation, I went down to Putney Bridge Theatre in a horse 'bus, in order to see him in *The Red Lamp*. I remember it was very hot, and how we bumped over the cobbles as I sat tightly clasping a bunch of red roses which I sent round to him as an offering, but which unfortunately got given to his wife instead! I know Lily Brayton was acting with him, and I thought I detected him eyeing her over-admiringly, and was appallingly jealous!

Well, the miracle had happened, and here was I now again bumping along the same road by the side of my adored one. It was then that he confided to me the story of his second establishment, the lady of which I did not meet for some years. She had seen him in *The Dancing Girl* when but seventeen, and had fallen in love with him. She also had written to him, and begged for a meeting which he had declined. She wrote again. He went to Marienbad taking with him, as he always did, a pile of unanswered letters to be sorted. Hers was included. He threw it on the fire and went out for a walk. When he came back, among the charred paper her address remained unconsumed – on such a chance hangs one's destiny. He changed his mind and wrote to her. In the end they met, and before long she was the mother of his boy; since then she had given up her life entirely to him. There were other children; and of course he visited her as often as possible. He felt himself tied to her by the most unbreakable ties – marriage one can escape from, but not a responsibility of honour like that.

He was on his way to see her now. He thought it his duty to tell me, that I should know. The world for me grew blacker than the darkness round us. Here indeed was a barrier between us which all my tenacity would never break down. We drew up at a gateway through which I could see a long one-storeyed house standing back in a garden. He bade me good night, paid the cabman to drive me back to London, and using his latch-key, disappeared within the building.

The cab rumbled slowly off with me. No doubt the other lady was already in his arms. I cried in an indescribable agony of grief all the way back – sitting huddled up in the corner, a miserable little black-clothed figure, feeling tragically lonely, in face of my first big encounter with the fire of life. But that night, which I spent mostly stretched on the floor, I fought through somehow to resignation. I accepted the inevitable. I would not be jealous or mean-spirited. This lady was part of him – the mother of his children. He cared for her, and what he cared for, I must of necessity care for too. Love that was not great enough for this was no real love.

Her father now dead, Olivia must have felt she could win her mother over to a more sympathetic view of her passion:

December 12   Efford Park, Lymington

My dearest Aunt Judy,

For your charming and sympathetic letter many thanks. The most astonishing and dramatic incident of all has now taken place – on the very night I arrived home I told Mother everything!!!!!!!!!! – !! *How* I did it – or exactly *why* I did it – heaven knows – She took it like a brick – I could not have believed that even *she* could be so sensible – had I but dreamed it I should have told her long ago, and avoided all the treacherous deceit which has so ill repaid the goodness of such a mother – I read her his letters and some of mine – and from the first she was overcome at the beauty of his conduct, which she rightly declared to be that of one man in a thousand – to clear him was all I desired, mindful ever of his words 'Whatever you do, do not let her think badly of me' – myself I made no attempt to exonerate – she termed my behaviour 'disgusting', and I was content to leave it so. I cannot expect other people to look at things in the same way that I do – viz. that a womans pride should be her armour against all the world but one man – and to him it should be her sacrifice – then so few understand how to love, mercifully he looks at things from the same point of view as myself – tho' she cannot realize that. I could not have believed that anybody *could* so completely place themselves outside the maternal role. I talk quite freely about him to her now, and call him by his Christian name – She is going to let me see his plays – even take me up specially for the first night of 'Nero' – and also see him occasionally when she is present – and as, after our last meeting I should not have felt inclined to continue those kind of relations with him – the arrangement seems very satisfactory. She goes so far as to hope that if he sees more of me, he will fall in love with me, as she thinks it very sad he does not return the passion!! isn't she *extraordinary*?!! – she *will* have it that he would never marry his chère amie – but I think she is mistaken – he has very strong ideas on the subject, not like other men . . .

For five years I had now been pursuing the object of my adoration, and still there were no signs of any diminution in my ardour. Again Herbert wrote and asked my mother to see him, and she met him at the house of a friend to discuss what had best be done about it. This time I did not accompany her, but they agreed that restraint and opposition were more likely to fan than to extinguish the flame, and that I had better be left to do as I liked. I expect he assured my mother that I should be safe in his hands – (perhaps 'arms' would have been more appropriate) – and so I was, as far as his will and intention went, when I did not try him past human endurance!

Her mother's report on the interview was duly passed on to Miss Mackay in a letter of December 21st:

. . . Mother duly returned – of course quite knocked up. She is somewhat vague about the famous interview – I can get little of her impressions of him out of her beyond that – he is a very 'nice old thing' and she is 'very sorry for him' and that he gave her the idea of a new hatched chick!!! They apparently got on very well and both carried it thro' gracefully – tho' the whole absurdity nearly caused them to choke! He appears to have said every imaginable charming thing about me – thinks I am pretty – clever and witty with a wonderful sense of humour – a marvellously exalted mind – and an extraordinary letter writer! So if I'm not unbearably vain – I don't know who will be! he was a darling and on Mother mentioning the Brookie episode [I can throw no light on this, but it probably refers to the actor Charles Brookfield] – pooh poohed it as nothing – which was dear of him after the row he made about it! Did I ever tell you, I saw that famous individual in a bus on the Monday?!! wasn't it a queer coincidence because it had caused friction with Herbert   I could hardly bring myself to be civil to him!! Herbert also desired me to know Viola to whom in a rash moment he seems to have confided part of 'l'affaire'!! so odd to retail ones love romances to ones daughter – and *so* like him! alas! daughters generally have bosom friends! I ask nothing better – she has always been very dear to me as you know and Mother makes no objection. She is going to ask the bon monsieur to lunch and I write now when I like – so I have scored all round – a *splendid* woman is she not? He did not like the miniature   said the mouth was wrong – well – he should know better than most people!! How curiously those two must have regarded each other – she the being her child had chosen before all the world – he the mother of one who has given herself to him – they parted on excellent terms after about an hour.

1906

When Olivia and her mother came up to London they usually stayed with a cousin, Minnie Bodley (wife of the well-known architect, C. F. Bodley) who had a house in Gloucester Place. On this occasion, however, of which the highlight was to be the opening night of Tree's Nero, they made use of an hotel.

26 January 1906   York Hotel, Albemarle Street

Dearest Aunt Judy,
         Thank God it is all over! – the suspense of the last days was something unbearable – I came up Saturday and went to 'The Enemy of the People' – worse luck tho' things went quite quietly and Herbert did not send for me – he was in tremendous form however – and I am still firm in the opinion that nothing on earth could beat the 'Man Who Was'. I stayed in bed next morning and at three Herbert came in answer to a telegram!! – He was very very, mad – and very very dear – we had just a minute or two to ourselves – after that he recited a piece out of 'Nero' – plunging into it with all his soul   his face playing as it does on the stage – it was so odd to see this man in London rig rendered bizarre by uncut hair and a peacock blue tie! – raving of dying, red mullets and nightingales tongues – !!! His visit of course lifted me to the seventh heaven with the result that my brilliance entirely captivated a youth who dined that night! Monday – I tried to shop but was too distrait to succeed. In the evening we went to Bernard Shaw's 'Major Barbara' which is one of the cleverest things imaginable . . .
         Yesterday was perfectly hideous – true in one thing I was made happy – Mother went to her doctor about an internal pain which has worried me nearly silly lately – he finds it is a strained kidney – probably from lifting the General – and with care all will get right – which is a mercy.
         The rest of the time I was quite beside myself and after nearly fainting in Harrods had to come home. It seemed interminable ages till the evening but it came at last. I had my hair dressed and a delightful new gown and

looked as well as anybody could who was ill with anxiety. We had a box – but saw quite abominably   having to kneel to do so at all. It was a brilliant house – and Herbert's stepmother was opposite us – a dear old lady – doubtless you saw a list of the other people. As for the play it is truly gorgeous. One banqueting scene particularly reaching a very high level of art – but I do not concur with Herbert in thinking it was the most wonderful thing ever done. 'The Darling of the Gods' and 'Ulysses' were both greater pieces of staging – *the* thing of the evening was his Nero which is undoubtedly one of the finest of his many fine roles – there is a breadth – a sympathy – an inspiration in it that are amazing – nothing could exceed the perfection of his facial play – especially when snarling at Mrs Tree. He looks so young and handsome too – the robes were quite indescribable – tho' Mother says they were like nightgowns!! Those of Madame were the richest – her acting was very passable – but to give her the role [Agrippina] was an insult! It was very well received – and is making for a big success. God knows how thankful I am – failure would have meant ruin – and of that I dare not even think. I did not see him tho' he looked at me – and he rang me up on the telephone as soon as I got back! – wasn't it *sweet* of him? for ages he had never been to bed – and was quite knocked up – at the very last he forgot every word of his part – and the prompter nearly went frantic! He also sweated so the carmine of the roses on his head ran onto his cheeks!! – poor *angel*!! Of course I told him how divine I thought it all – and then went upstairs and fainted with variations of hysterics!! – the strain was over at last. Today I feel very tired but very happy – as all the papers – which I had started fussing over before seven! – are so polite.

Mother and I went to tea with him at the theatre and Max was there! We were very glad to meet and made great friends – he thinks I am very pretty – I certainly looked rather nice!! – I then shunted Mother on to him – and my lord who looked very well in spite of everything and had had his hair cut – and I made love!! He told me several things which made me very happy – he always wears the pencil I gave him and last night he wore the letter I wrote to wish him luck – next to his heart – strange thought when his wife was leaning there! He made me the proud possessor of one of his Nero rings which hangs on my bracelet this moment – isn't it interesting – just to be worn by him once on such a first night!!! His other woman is behaving so badly that he is beginning to fall in love with me!!!! She *is* such a devil! is *furious* he succeeded and she calls herself in love with him! We finished up with chocolate at the Carlton – and so ended the most interesting hour I have ever spent. Oh! how glad – how thankful – how grateful I am! Mother was dear and charming – but doesn't like his rooms much. Tomorrow we go down to see a house near Bath – and

Sunday home. I think this is the first week I have not heard from you – it seems so odd but suppose as I had no news last time and you were busy and probably had none you did not think it worth while – don't fail Sunday tho'. London is dirty as ever! – I am not quite fit. Must go to bed – so bon soir my dear – believe me

Most joyously your,
O.M.T.

In the following extract from a letter of February 8th, there was evidently a proposal for Olivia's eldest brother Ivor to sell Herbert a car – and also a reference to Maud Tree's affaire with the matinée idol Lewis Waller:

. . . Ivor came but motoring was perfectly glacial! He is trying to sell Herbert a car – I settled up an interview and he went to see him, but said my lord was too absent minded for anyone to get any sense out of him! absent minded or not he sees and takes in twice as much as most people! – I expect he looked somewhat curiously on *my* brother!! I do not wonder you and Herbert complain of my orthography – it is enough to knock you flat in my novel – all pure carelessness! . . . Max is a beast – he has not answered my truly charming epistle! . . . I am also *assured* that madame put it well within my lords power to divorce her over Lewis Waller – when he was acting there she moved her dressing room next to his. Herbert sent for her 'This is *too* disgusting – do you want the whole theatre to look on you as nothing but a common harlot?' clever as ever she put on a winning smile 'oh! Herbie dear – what *is* a harlot?'!!!!! Mon dieu qu'on parle! O.M.T.

In the spring following my father's death, my mother and I went to Italy, staying in Rome and Florence. I do not remember where my first meeting with Max took place, but that it had preceded our going abroad is evident from these letters of his:

21 February 1908*   48 Upper Berkeley Street

Dear Miss Truman,
        I really am appalling – and appalled. Is it really three weeks since you sent me the books and a delightful letter *and* the not less delightful criticisms? It seems only yesterday –
        Your praises of my books made me so vain and happy that time has flown

* Max appears to have written 1908 in mistake for 1906. In fact he seldom dated his letters at all, beyond giving the day of the week.

with wings of lightning; and it seems almost premature to thank you now. Here, however, are my very many thanks indeed; and the books, in a registered parcel; and also my very many congratulations on the way you write:— the vivacity of your style and the unerring rightness of your judgement (whenever you are judging *me*, at any rate!)

Do tell me how your novel is getting on. I look forward to the novel. Lucky young person, to be getting away from England next week! I can hardly bear to hear of people leaving England while I have to remain. I should like all the harbours closed till I were free to go too. All the same, I hope you will have a very nice time.

Kindest regards to your mother.

Yours very sincerely,
Max Beerbohm

Wednesday   48 Upper Berkeley Street

Dear Olivia,

As you call me Max, I suppose I can call you Olivia. My hair is already rather grey at the temples: not that there is anything very premature about that; for I am thirty-three years old. Dr Primrose [a reference to *The Vicar of Wakefield*] called his daughter Olivia. Why should not I address you similarly?

If you would rather be called Miss Truman, call me Mr Beerbohm; and I will revert to my previous custom. I would have written to you sooner; only I have been hoping against hope that I *might* be able to be at His Majesty's on Thursday. I had promised to go away to stay with some people in the country from to-day till the end of the week. And there was just the chance that this visit might get itself postponed. I have made efforts; but the efforts are in vain: I have to go away to-day. Most unwillingly. I would have been such a delight to see you again. Shall you have started for Italy when I return? And, if so, when shall you be in London again? If you will send me the MS of your novel, I think I can get a capable revisionist for you, though I don't fancy there is any real need for him. Please pity me tomorrow evening. I, in the depths of Warwickshire, shall be pitying myself very much indeed.

Yours,
Max (Beerbohm)

48 Upper Berkeley Street

Dear Olivia,

No: I shan't call you anything but Olivia. Olivia is a very pretty name; much prettier than Prig – even than Priggie; and Olivia you remain, so far as I am concerned. The name suits you. I mean that its prettiness more or less counteracts, mitigates, and dulcifies the extraordinary personal plainness with which the gods have handicapped you. You say you look better in the evening. Possibly. But *how much* better? That is the point. Barring a radical transformation, I shall have to go on thinking of you as Olivia even when we meet in the evening. (These are not 'pointed little shafts', are they? But what you call 'blugeons', and what *I* call 'bludgeons'.) I have just written to your mother, saying I shall be much delighted to lunch on Wednesday. Some day I shall ask her to bring you to dinner with me. You cannot imagine how radiantly beautiful I look in evening dress. Plain black cloth, and a simple insertion of white linen over the bosom; but the effect is divine, they tell me.

I do so look forward to receiving the novel: it shall be taken great care of, and all your instructions shall be obeyed to the letter.

So till Monday, Olivia,

> Yours,
> Max Beerbohm

At this time both Herbert and Max were almost equally attracted by Olivia, as her next letter (of March 12th) testifies:

My dearest Aunt Judy,

So sorry not to write last week but I positively did not have a moment. I went to 'Nero' Tuesday night – Herbert gave me the royal box which included the royal room – my cousin [probably Mrs Minnie Bodley] and Miss Johnston [a former governess] chaperoned me but being both discreet women, I saw the good man 3 times alone, when we kissed and hugged to our hearts delight! Next day we lunched with Max at Princes – (I provided a man for Mother) – and we had a rare time. He is a perfect dear and I got no end of family information out of him which it would have taken me years to extract from his brother – and he is going to help me no end with my book which he has at present – Herbert was *wildly* jealous of him, and I had to give him a tremendous talking to as I won't have that kind of rot, where upon he shut up. He popped in to see me in the evening with Max – who is much épris – in attendance and popped out again as quickly – to go to Putney!! . . . Thursday we lunched with Herbert at the Carlton – and afterwards got about 10 minutes alone, which we naturally made the most of – he *is* violent!! He then gave me seats at a deadly matinee at the Savoy, where I sat with my maid in the stalls, and he in another womans box and never took his eyes off me! We then drove back together! . . . Friday night I took Ivor to 'Nero' and saw Herbert twice – but only for a minute by himself – it was of course souvenir night, and he signed all ours. He *would* look at me as if he wanted to eat me up – he simply gives the whole show away – and Ivor has fairly hooked on to it – tells Mother she is an awful fool, that she ought to shut me up in the country with no money ect: but she knows me well enough to be aware that while she trusts me, she muzzles me – what a horrible – what a disgraceful thing it would be were I to take advantage of her leniency in letting me see and write to him, to betray her – I think she would never forgive herself. If she had put pressure on I should have bolted – as it is she has drawn me closer to her than ever – Dieu but she is a clever woman – so clear sighted – not a bit tête-monté like me. Saturday I went to see a perfectly *deadly* skit on 'Nero' at the Coliseum and then he came in for a few minutes to say good-bye. He was simply worn out and very down in his luck – and it was a very touching party all round – and I felt monstrously miserable afterwards, and wept and wrote to him with his coat tails still in sight!! Lor'! how little in Springfield days [Springfield was the house in Taplow where Miss Mackay had been Olivia's governess] did I dream of laying my head on that august shoulder! Putney has been behaving better to him lately – and he runs off from me to her with avidity – an extraordinary man! . . .

It was whilst we were in Italy that I received both a telegram, and a letter from Herbert, which at last showed a touch of real intimacy. *Incidentally, this is the first of a long line of letters from Tree to Olivia with no greeting. By this simple device he could express his warmest sentiments without compromising himself.*

6 April 1906   His Majesty's Theatre

It has been a great joy to have your delightful letters and to know that you are seeing the world happily. Forgive my not writing to you, but I always feel that when I do write, I must sit down with some solid hours in front of me in order to express my gratitude at sufficient length. Your letters are always interesting and enthralling, while your spelling affords me that occasional 'comic relief' without which life were too strenuous a business.

Indeed, indeed you are helpful to me, for you flatter me into self-esteem, and what better incentive to striving can be given to man? I hope this letter will still reach you at Florence, if not no doubt it will be forwarded to you. I am sorry your brother should think as he does, perhaps you will tell him that I am not without a tender consideration for you, and that my influence has not been a malign one.

. . . I am just told that I must descend to the lower regions, so I will say good night for to-night. I will try to write again to-morrow. God bless you my sweet friend.

Yours,
H.B.T.

Before we returned the news came that Herbert's brother Julius had died, which was a great blow to him. He was playing in *Hamlet* when we got to London, and in view of his recent loss the grave scene affected him greatly, and I wept in sympathy with him. Max answered my letter of condolence as follows:

Dear Olivia,

I have been away and have just come back and found your very kind and sweet letter of sympathy. (That other letter, written from Italy, never reached me: I wonder what became of it; I suppose the Italian Government treated it as one of the works of art which they will not allow to cross the frontier.) But thank you so much for this other letter. The death of my brother has been a grief indeed to all us Beerbohms. He was the oddest and most delightful of men, and we were all so fond of him: he kept us in a state of constant surprise and amusement, compassion, admiration, affection. And it is a large void where he was. I wish you had met him: you would have delighted in him.

Shall you be at home on Monday afternoon? Shall I come and see you about four o'clock? No 'blugeoning', believe me! A few vague suggestions, possibly, which you may as well ignore. I admire your novel immensely. You really are very gifted. I have begun to dislike you, as I haven't a beautiful nature. How have you, at your age – – – but I postpone my compliments till our meeting.

With kindest regards to your mother,

Ever yours,
Max Beerbohm

Then came anticipation of the first night of Colonel Newcombe.

May 16   Efford Park, Lymington

. . . And, as I told Herbert it is so odd coming back to everything here where no nook or glade but is full of past thoughts of him – I have been so very very close to him down here [Tree had not yet visited Efford: Olivia is referring to her own reveries] – there was once a time even when I disliked going to town because there people and things came between us and broke the link – I love a life so gentle and quiet that it can be entirely given up to him. But for the moment I am full of other ideas – the first night comes on apace – sprung on me quite suddenly for when I left town he had no idea when it would be. I am a prey as usual to alternate hopes and fears – it seems so mad a thing to take 'Nero' off with such houses – and yet so daring and independant that one cannot help admiring him for it and his contempt of the Golden Calf. I have been ploughing thro' all 4 vols: of the 'Newcomes' and have never been so excruciatingly bored! – but I have no doubt that well laced together by a clever dramatist – and acted with such pathos as I am sure Herbert will act it – it should be very fair – and it is magnificently cast thro'out – not the least neat allotment being that of the scolding shrewish little fiend, Mrs Mackenzie to Maude! – he is cruel that man for people will be sure to notice and talk. I am going up for it as I suppose I generally shall now – and we are going – my cousin and a man and Max – and doing a supper at the Carlton afterwards – it ought to be no end fun if only all goes well – otherwise – but I do not think of that. Max and I are closer friends than ever since he was blown up for making love, and he writes me the funniest letters on earth that make me simply *scream!* . . .

But the Daily Mail *attacked Tree. From Efford Park on May 20th Olivia wrote to Miss Mackay:*

. . . I am still suffering from the reaction from the frightful rage that treacherous article about Herbert in Wednesdays 'Daily Mail' threw me into – anything so low, so cowardly – so ridiculous I never read. I wrote a real stinger in reply to the 'Telegraph' but alas! they did not put it in   Herbert is in the most awful way over it – wrote piteously to me and wished to die – and I am in a horrible funk of the first night, as he seems quite panic struck – it is too *damnably* mean – I have done my level best to soothe and cheer the poor darling. You keep quite calm about Max – what does it matter if he *does* fall in love with me? . . .

I think Max was our guest several times that year, as is evidenced by his letters.

Tuesday   48 Upper Berkeley Street

Dear Olivia,

I have been really quite ill: feverish, head-acheish, in bed, taking remedies, desiring to die, etc., etc.; and have managed to crawl here, and am so far restored that I feel worthy to write to you. 'Kerslake and Dixon' are the names of my tailors, and 12 Hanover Street is their address. I tell you this, because you ask for the information; but I reject as false and grotesque your suggestion that I am 'the best dressed individual' that you know. That is what the Hottentot lady said to the missionary, and in her case the saying was a true one, no doubt. But coming from you to me, it won't do. I am neat and conscientious in costume: no more. Nor are K and D particularly brilliant artists. They do their best. By all means lead your brother to them, if he will go. But I expect he would prefer higher flights. I haven't heard from Herbert since he went to Marienbad – but I have no doubt he is enjoying himself very much there: he loves the place; and, though you may doubt it, he really is quite capable of looking after himself; he isn't half so vague as he seems; when it rains he seeks shelter under a tree or a roof; when food is placed before him he somehow manages to insert it into his mouth with a fork or a spoon; he always emerges undrowned from his morning bath; and never puts his coat on inside-out, or his hat on upside-down. Some good fairy watches over him all the time, believe me. Set your mind at rest. Of course he *may* be shipwrecked on the way home. But not even Viola, on whom you seem to pin your faith, could be of much help then. And she certainly would have been the reverse of helpful on dry land, had she accompanied him. He would have liked her to go; but you are wrong in imagining she could have saved him from the small worries of travel and exile. *She* really *is* thoroughly vague – doesn't know a boat from a train, or an hotel from a hill, and has never been cured of an unfortunate habit of wearing her gloves on her feet and her boots on her hands. She is a nice girl; but worse than useless for the duties you assign to her.

I do so look forward to the treat of coming again to Efford. May it be some time about the middle of August, do you think?

I haven't yet heard from Pinker; but have written to prod him. [Pinker seems to have been Max's literary agent, to whom he had sent Olivia's MS.]

Please give my best remembrances to your mother.

Yours ever,
Max

Meanwhile Olivia kept Miss Mackay au fait with the progress of her 'Tree habit'.

. . . I went up to 'Capt: Swift' yesterday [May 22] – and also caught a glimpse of Evelyn who was very festive after an awful go of toothache. They have a very nice tho' small house in Portman Street. It was an enormously smart matinee – but I don't care for Herbert in the role, which offended him very much! in any case he is too old and fat for it!!! – Afterwards we nearly had a most appalling quarrel, but didn't – (it is the only time I have ever been angry with him) – instead of which he drove me down in enormous and most affectionate spirits to the station, where he introduced me to his dearest friend – a small and very ugly little parson!!! – he seems a dear tho' – Imagine me arriving with a very big actor and a very small parson – 'small', 'stock', and 'out' size! In two minutes Herbert gave the whole show away – but to the parson's credit be it said, he kept quite calm! My beloved got so excited at the moment of departure that he kissed his hand to me before the whole platform and two stolid Lymington worthies who happened to be on board!! – I am thankful to say he is happier in his mind tho' *fearfully* nervous – and I await the first night in an agony! . . .

Then came the first night of Colonel Newcombe.

1 June 1906   Efford Park, Lymington

Dearest Aunt Judy,

Well! Wasn't it all just *splendid*?! Oh! how the people stood by him and how they cheered – !! After the fall of the curtain on the first act I was simply so happy I didn't know what to do. It was an awfully smart house – and a whole crowd of pretty and well dressed women for a wonder – the usual first night lot were there – the Bancrofts, Kate Terry – Pinero, Mrs Langtry etc. Viola and Marjory Manners (who some people think I am like) in the Royal box – the former looking so nice in pale pink and pearls. My male cousin [Minnie Bodley's son, Hamilton] came with us and Max joined us in the middle of the second act – looking quite clean and jolly with my favourite tube roses in his buttonhole! As to what Herbert's acting was I cannot say – anything so simple, so dignified, so pathetic – is impossible to believe – there was not one false touch thro'out – hardly a dry eye remained at the end – tho' I was so overjoyed at his victory that I wasn't very sad! When he simply said 'I think we have won' – it was a great, great moment and I could have hugged all the gallery! The Daily Mail critic sat next to us – a nice looking young fellow rather – and do you know the devil who wrote that article was in the same row?!! My feelings were almost unbearable!! – when he saw that it was a success he got up and left the house . . .

After it was all over we all stumped onto the stage where the actors and actresses were receiving their friends. You know I have never been allowed 'behind' before and I was *so* fascinated! It is a *huge* stage – of course they were all still in costume and the highest of spirits! Then we four went on to the Carlton which was simply packed – and had a very pleasant little supper tho' the food was bad! – Herbert came and looked us up – and we stayed till about 12.45 when the lights were put out. Then we adjourned to where my lord and a party were feeding in a private room! The 'company' consisted of the adaptor and his wife – rather awful looking – the Felix Semons – the King's doctor – he tells long stories and forgets the points – he has a very strong German accent – and Gill the divorce counsel – Maxine Elliot, the American actress – very handsome – Marion Terry – who was charming to me – I am going to see her on Sunday when she comes to Lymington for the night – Claude Lowther – who has so often wanted to meet me on hearing my letters but little suspected that I was the writer – a great blagueur – Norman Forbes – one of the actors of the evening – Forbes Robertson's brother and the creator of the irresistably funny original Sir Andrew Aguecheek most witty and nice – and of course Herbert – and Herbert's wife!!!!

I have had the honour of seeing two of his mistresses and various of his progeny but perhaps none interested me as deeply as Maude – a charming, amusing and fascinating lady I found her – and we hit it off perfectly – she rather liked me – told me I was the image of Brown Potter when she came to town first and seeing my look of amazed horror hastened to add that I needn't mind as she was a very beautiful woman too!! Everybody agreed!!!! [Brown Potter, the American actress and friend of Edward VII, when Prince of Wales, had inspired this limerick by Tree: There was a young lady Brown Potter/Who quitted the land that begot her/In all winds and weathers she wore but three feathers/And adopted 'Ich dien' as her motter.] Poor lady – how she would have hated me if she had known what I was to her husband – I am very glad I have always stuck up for her – I only wish I could really do something material – but no power in heaven or earth will ever draw those two together again . . . I wish I could be her friend but it would not do – she would turn and rend me – however fond she were of me, if she found out I had so much as touched Herbert's little finger – and then I suppose to eat her salt and betray her husband would not be quite! – I do tho' respect myself – that tho' she stands between me and my only possible source of happiness – I do not hate her and am not jealous of her – Max ragged me to death and as the baby of the party kept calling for buns and milk for me! We did not break up till nearly 3!! I don't know when I have enjoyed myself so much. Minnie – impayable as ever thought Max 'very gentlemanly'.

Next day . . . Max came to tea – but fled when he found Minnie ensconced!! Thursday I shopped and did the Academy – which is worse than ever and then – I went to see Herbert – We sent Evelyn into the next room – and for half an hour nearly we were alone together – he signed me 15 souvenirs among other things!! The result of that interview is that now nothing but a mere shadow stands between us – he is to all intents and purposes my absolute master – I cannot say that it has made any difference in my relation to him – from the first kiss he ever gave me – I have felt myself in some strange way, his mistress – how far I am morally guilty heaven knows, but it seemed to me yesterday that he but exercised a right all along his – not since I have loved him but since his lips touched mine – what happened was certainly not my fault for the moment for as ever – all passion died in his arms. God guards me thus I think – how else explain my almost repulsion for it – when the means are there – to gratify a desire with which I sometimes ache for days? – I was simply passive, he thought, cold – but of course the whole blame is mine – I who have schemed, and planned and worked to gain some power over him – ever decking out my body – suggesting – tempting, alluring – he is a man, and a sensual man – I am pretty, above all I am fresh and young – I give him a love and an abandonment to turn a saint's head – and if at last I have turned his – as ever the woman is to blame – I believe in 9 cases out of 10 – the world is right to condemn her and extenuate the man – we are devils. We use the highest and most sacred means to attain our ends – we are worse than vicious we are hypocrites – to God, to ourselves, to the men we love – we have no more reverence in choosing our weapons than a Jesuit – that is what I am today – no better and no worse than most of my wretched sex . . .

This theme is continued in a letter of June 6th:

. . . accidents can hardly occur with someone sitting in the next room!! – but you cannot always ask me to have my kissing personally supervised! as to not relying on my own strength – you need have no fear   I have never experianced the faintest inclination to lose my head in his presence – when I do, it will be a different thing. I said nothing but shadow stands between us – I mean nothing but the *strict* technicality, described I believe in the divorce court – as 'sexual intercourse'!!! according to law, no preliminary canter counts – you may say morally it does but I think not more than the original kiss   you need have no fear – remember *his mistress cannot become his wife* – come what may I must have that supreme advantage over Putney should Maude die – besides it is so much easier to rule a man whose desire you have whetted and left unsatisfied, than if you have surrendered – the crudity of all this is appalling – but the fancy has taken me not to lie and pretend for once. You seem to imagine *I* took the initiative in love making – you are wrong – I am too truly a member of my snaky sex – we lead men on and on into a cul-de-sac where there is no opening – and then we stop short, so that when they take the one path left them, we may make a scene and talk about *their* having betrayed us – we press the spring – but we take very good care it is they who speak the guilty words – we plan the crime and make them the crimnel – 'The woman tempted me' was spoken in days before chivalry obtainted and the truth was spoken – we have tempted Adam ever since – as far as I can see we shall continue to as long as we possess what G.B.S. chooses to baldly name the 'life force'.

Are you calmer now you know I am no worse than I was when you saw me – and in no greater danger? It is no good wishing I had never seen him – he is a good man in a way and has done me good. I should undoubtidly have followed my calling anyhow and lured someone else, who might have done me harm – Au fond, as far as a woman can be, I am unsullied – for the most we poor creatures can hope, is to remain mistresses of ourselves and the situation – and that I am – and if I carry that, and a few good works to heaven, I have no doubt an all understanding Diety will still pardon him, for me.

For the rest Mother gets on – if slowly – and the weather is divine. I trust it will restore your shattered nerves – and not cause you to doubt either the honesty or the love of her who has the honor to subscribe herself

Olivia

However Max also was still in pursuit. As for the fiasco of Tree's non-arrival, recounted with such feeling towards the end of this letter, we are to hear Tree's version of this and to follow his attempts to bring the visit off in subsequent letters.

July 5   Efford Park, Lymington

Dearest Aunt Judy,

Well – the great Max party duly came off – and I think was very successful – he is a dear and witty – especially à deux. We did nothing

49

special just croquet and pow wow and on Sunday he and I read to each other most of the afternoon. He most conscientiously admired all I did singing – writing – recitation etc.!! He was awfully sweet and did me a couple of very delightful caricatures – he did not however stop there but would insist on kissing one – and the fearful thing is I allowed him to, not once but twice!! He has such quaint views on it – can see no more in it than shaking hands!! The secret of my apparently bad conduct however is simple – his touch – that extraordinary cool vital skin, is exactly like Herbert's and fascinated me so that I could not help myself – I should have liked him to go on holding my hand for ages and to have shut my eyes and pretended it was my dearest!! All the time he was here the thought that he was of Herbert's flesh and blood attracted me – and made me want to touch him – and I was always on the watch for some feature or intonation like his brothers – and jumping when they came – However I thought that it was being unfair on him and when he wanted to kiss me before he went – I told him no, because Herbert wouldn't like it. He was *awfully* dashed poor little dear! – he wears simply ravishingly cut clothes. Wasn't it too dreadful – Herbert wired to say he was coming next day – of course I never slept at all and got up about 7 to see after his room – (his bed caused me the wildest emotion!!!) he never came – knowing how mad he is we thought nothing of it – in the end it turned out that he started at 9.30 – got to Winchester – broke down – couldn't get on and after wasting a whole precious day and coming 70 miles had to go back!! Wasn't it simply damnable luck? however I believe he is coming Sunday or the beginning of next week – I am dying to see him again and he says ditto!! I went to the rottenest bazaar in Lymington yesterday – and today – perhaps in conse-quence am on the sick list – We expect Mrs Powell [presumably a family friend] in a minute or two. I enclose you a perfectly excellent snapshot of my august self and one of the three of us!

With my father out of the way, I had no difficulty in persuading my mother to invite the great actor to stay with us, nor did he show any reluctance to accept, though it proved rather difficult to fulfil. Efford was a great distance from London, Herbert was playing regularly, always up to his eyes not only with the business of his theatre, and plans for future productions, but with outside engagements, and two families to consider. I must have been a considerable attraction to him to cause him to add to this burden. At last he announced his arrival, and putting on my best dress – I rather think the eighteenth-century absurdity – I set off to meet him in the carriage and pair. What was my misery when he failed to appear. In the following letter he explains the reason, though I am not sure how the motor comes into it; still it was very characteristic of him to try and come the way he was not expected. It is interesting that he refers to my friend Evelyn Alexander, so soon to die. Actually 'Cockie' Alexander* and his own two younger daughters became intimates, having been schoolfellows.

I am terribly sorry about Sunday. I started for your destination at 9.30 and broke down about 30 miles from it. I could find no means of reaching you and was compelled to return to London in another car, reaching there just in time for dinner. I was greatly disappointed, as you may imagine, but I will not fail to come to you next week – possibly next Sunday.

I saw Max last night, he appears to have enjoyed his visit to you hugely. I wrote you a letter some days ago, and hope you got it. I have not heard from you since. I hope there was nothing in it to annoy you. Thank your mother, please, for her kind little note, and tell her how disappointed I was. Do please write me another letter in your own pretty way. I get the flowers and wear them every night. Is it not possible for you to see the play before we take it off? I suppose not. Shall I send Miss Alexander some tickets? We are very busy rehearsing 'A Winter's Tale', but I am looking forward to the holiday which is looming.

As I write I am called away – do write to me,

Yours ever,
H.B.T.

His reference to the German editors is in connection with the invitation he had received from the Kaiser to visit Berlin. His pleasure about this may have been a little due to the 'call of the blood' as his uncle, General von Unruh, had been aide-de-camp to the Kaiser's grandfather.

I am just snatching a few minutes before the play to write to tell you that you may rely on my paying you a visit before leaving London. I hope it may be this week – or Sunday – in the latter case, I suppose I should motor down with Max.

I always revel in your sweet, kind letters. I seem someone different from the self which the rest of the world knows, and it is pleasant (is it not?) not to be oneself! – or to be really oneself, and for no one to know, except one's other self! and therefore not to be oneself but by proxy!

* Evelyn's younger sister, and a celebrated prankster.

No, I am not worried about Newcome, but I really need a holiday, it is immensely appreciated by the stalls, but the pit stay away. I think they don't quite understand the pathos of it all – the pathos of not making a fuss – to bear misfortune without rancour – *that* is the real pathos; some of the meaner mortals leave off flattering God by ceasing to say their prayers when things don't go smoothly.

We had a great 'to-do' with the German editors, it was a delightful experience, and we were all very gay and so were they. I don't know whether you read a little speech I made for the poor children at the Mansion House the other day, but you are so sympathetic to my little words that you won't mind my repeating these: I said: 'Charity is only the conscience-money that we pay to the poor – we give them by courtesy what is theirs by right.'

Yes, I shall do Newcome again in the Autumn – certainly on tour – I wonder whether you will see it then.

Thursday

Thus far I had written on Monday, and since then I have been constantly trying to switch on to you again, but alas, there has been a run upon me, and I have been busy with the preparations for Winter's Tale. I do not yet know whether I am bringing Max along on Sunday, or whether I shall postpone my visit until later, but I reiterate my promise to come to you. I will write to you again to-morrow if I possibly can.

Thank you for the beautiful flowers which arrive daily, I long to see you again.

Good night.

Yours ever,
Herbert B. Tree

In the end he *did* turn up, though even then several hours late, since he went by train to Salisbury and motored from there to Lymington – a slightly circuitous route – not arriving till about 9 o'clock. On this occasion I had got myself up in a princess dress of white muslin with mauve bows on the shoulders and ribbon to match in my hair, which had inspired Max to make me a delightful drawing of Napoleon standing on St Helena – a few strokes with a quill pen, and inscribed 'To Josephine'. After Herbert had had some supper, I took him out into the garden, which was really rather a beautiful one, with long glades of trees, walks of rhododendrons and azaleas, and an alley bordered by yew hedges known as the Lovers' Walk – which seemed the obvious place to lead him. It must have been a perfect summer's night, for I know the stars were shining, and that I wore no wrap over my thin dress. At the end of the alley was a seat, and there we sat, my head on his shoulder, perhaps the most purely happy half hour I have spent on this earth, slightly degraded by my mother eventually calling us in; evidently she mistrusted too much starlight and artistic temperament when in conjunction.

He had, of course, to go back to London next day. It seemed almost incredible that, beginning as a child belonging to a world utterly alien to his, my years of devotion should at last have been crowned by the triumph of his actually sleeping under our roof! He was then about 52, slightly putting on weight, his colouring too sandy, his face too full for really good looks, but his height, his carriage, his manner at once authoritative and debonair, gave him tremendous distinction. I was so overwhelmed by his presence, and my attitude to him so much that of a worshipper, that the details I long to recall escape me. I feel sure that for days after his visit I must have walked on air. However my everyday life of idle busyness must have gone on: the comings and goings of neighbours, the games of croquet with my mother – the only game I have ever played well – the readings aloud; the drives into Lymington; the large meals.

There follows Olivia's description of the visit at the time:

July 14   In the train

Dearest Aunt Judy,
          Mon dieu! how much has happened since I took up pen to indite to you last!! – On Tuesday morning Herbert wired that unless he did so again he would be down by the 4.50 – I spent a day of palpitating terror (sents tu mon coeur?!!) the telegraph boy became an apparition of dreadfulness to me – he did not come however – with emotion choked heart I went to the station – and neither did Herbert either! – I was dashed as you know only I can be dashed – but with the courage of dispair I faced this the greatest of my many disappointments – with perfectly calm face – if set and white – I drove up to the door and there Mother handed me a telegram from him – saying that he had missed the train – was going to Salisbury and had sent for a motor to bring him over – the fearful joy of this new development overcame me – I fled and howled – after a while I calmed down – cooled my nose and garbed myself slightly, but beautifully. At 9.30 I was convulsively clasping his hand on the door step!!!

How exquisite a compliment – this coming to me at any distance and any cost – what an example of his unalterable will when he means a thing! I gave him supper – a little constranidly – for the man was there but with what rapture! – afterwards there was a short time in the drawing room – with he at his most brilliant and charming – when he ignored Mrs Powell (who has become unsufferably boring) with that polite thoroughness so uniquely his. Then she went to bed – and we into the garden – how wonderful it seems to think of that wander in the darkness under the stars in the still, sweet smelling night – moments without regret – without desire – without past or future – divine happiness – I just lay in his arms with his lips on mine – in silence – which is the most perfect communion of all – ultimately we returned to earth and the house, and he recited to us – Oh but so marvellously! the low thrilling voice, the ever changing eyes, the mobile face, the small facile gestures!! and then I recited to him – of which on the whole he approved – my action is too marked – Then I took him to my sitting room and showed him all his pictures and relics – so big he looked in my little den! I kept him till I dared no longer – and then – it was nearly 2 – put him to bed. As for me – I had no inclination to sleep and sleep I did not – but dwelt on the delight of my realized dreams – that now I can picture him actually, where I have pictured him a thousand times a day in imagination – heavens *how* I have lived for it! Being awake I was up betimes to see Mrs Powell off by the first train – and then in the most perfect teagown and the servants being at breakfast I went in to him!! I see your hair rising dear lady – but remember what I have told you – that now there are no bars between us – it was my perfect right – I just kissed him – and sat on his bed a few minutes – and went – it was a very precious moment to me.

When we were up and dressed we went for another ramble in the woods and garden – very lovely but not as the night before for he was a trifle distrait – Then we breakfasted and immediately afterwards – started in his car which had come down over night – for London. Nearly 4½ hours we were on the road alone together even as husband and wife might be – and to me who have never been with him for one hour and a half it was paradise – as hand in hand we flew! We arrived in the end alas! – and I went at once to sleep the sleep of the exhausted wicked! – In the evening I dined with Stella and Sweetie at the Hyde Park and went on to a box Herbert had given me at the Court for Bernard Shaw's 'You Never Can Tell' which is perfectly excellent – so clever, amusing and well acted – my friend Louis Calvert being as perfect as ever. Thursday I slept most of the morning and shopped in the afternoon – going on to tea at the Carlton, which was packed, and where we were to have met Herbert, but he ran into a brougham and smashed up his car – so never came. I'm dreadfully frightened at his going in the things. Instead we went to dine with him at the theatre. I, in all my ball finery – Miss Collier was there when we arrived

– but had to go on – she is one of the most charming women imaginable. Herbert was most appallingly down in his luck – not at all well – very much worried – and recalling some very tragic past incidents which he told me of – till I was simply wild with misery to see him so suffer and be able to do nothing . . .

His next letter to me came from Marienbad, always his most loved holiday resort, and shows that the Lovers' Walk had not been without result on our intimacy.

July 21   Gruenes Kreuz, Marienbad

Thank you for your dear letters, and for all your kind, unselfish thoughts. I can only blush at my unworthiness of them, but believe me, I feel infinite encouragement in knowing that there is a large soul 'thinking of me'. Indeed, indeed I understand all you say, and value each word you give me. Yes, it would be lovely if you were here. Why did not your mother contract some trivial ailment that she might be ordered here? . . . Since you wish to know about my health, I think I am really much better, though I often worry about home affairs, and have awful nightmares – realities tortured into shapeless phantoms, but the morning comes and laughter. It is lovely of you to say you would like to send flowers to my dear friend, and show your large and generous nature in other ways, but I do not think that it would be quite right that you should do this now. I mean not right in the eyes of others, and one must consider these things. But I do thank you with all my heart. I will tell you more when we meet again, which I hope may be soon!

That handcuff [we hear more about this in a later letter] – I have been thinking it will be better to postpone it until my return – do you not think that 1½ inches would be a little unbecoming on the wrist? and then I don't know whether it would have to be cut in order to put on. I will think of some pretty inscription – I have an idea. Have you heard from Max? I hear he has written a very clever article in the 'Saturday'.

Please give my kindest regards to your mother and thank her for her great kindness in letting me come to your delightful home. I suppose the roses are still in bloom? . . . do write me when you have spare time, although I often reproach myself for taking up your precious time and allowing you to concentrate yourself upon me and my affairs. God bless you, my dear, kind friend whose grateful servant I shall ever be.

                                                          H.B.T.

On his return from abroad I tried to get him to take 'the mixture as before', but it would seem that my brother Billy* was now showing his disapproval of the whole affair, and two of Herbert's next letters prove his reluctance to intrude where he might be unwelcome.

I am delighted to get your letter to-day – it was quite natural you should write as you did. Since I have been back – I returned yesterday week – I have been fearfully busy with these preparations, hence my silence. Yes, I hope I may be able to come this week. I am just having the geography examined and may be able to pay you a visit on Sunday (or Saturday) motoring on to another place . . .

You appear to hear very queer accounts of me. And what about your brother? I should not like to come unless I felt I was welcome to all your people. I daresay you will understand this. If you really believe me to be other than some of your friends describe me, you will tell him, will you not? Though indeed I fully understand a brother's solicitude for his sister. You need have no fear about telling me anything, for nothing can make any difference now, and I would like to be quite frank with you – I am, I think, acting wisely as well as rightly in doing what I am doing – and is no need for mystery on your side or mine. As regards yourself, you know, I hope, that I should put what is best for you before what is pleasant to me – that is the greater chivalry is it not? And I have at least not sought the kindness and the devotion you have honoured me with – from which no harm has come. Oh, it is difficult, is it not? I will tell you all about Marienbad, when we meet.

Believe me ever,

Yours sincerely,
H.B.T.

At this point light relief is provided by a letter from Max in his most inimitable style, evidently referring to Olivia's reaction to some criticism by him of the acting profession. The letter is dated August 9th.

My dear Olivia,

I have sent in my resignation to the editor of the 'Saturday Review', enclosing your letter, so that he shall understand exactly why I have taken the step. How blind I have been all these years! As you say, 'an attack on the stage in any form is, in his (Herbert's) great posistion, indirectly an

---

* Her favourite brother, Charles. All his friends, and Olivia too, called him Billy.

56

attack on him'. And to think I had never thought of that:— all the while that I was criticising this and that actor or theatre unfavourably I was incidentally stabbing Herbert in the back — lowering his profession in the eyes of the world, and thus lowering him. I can't forgive myself. Nothing can wipe out the hideous past. How he must have suffered. Yet he never uttered a groan. Well, I shall gnaw no longer at his vitals. The theatre will know me no more. Not the least painful part of the matter is that you — et tu Bruta — acknowledge as 'in the main true' what I said about the regrettableness of the public's attitude towards mimes in general. (*Mimes*, by the way, is a good old English word, not in the least derogatory; and used by me always to save the space that would be wasted by 'actors and actresses'. Give me another noun of common gender, and I will use that instead. But I forget: it is too late now.) 'In the main true'! Oh Olivia, say oh say that this was a slip of the pen. A treacherous private endorsement from you makes my crime seem doubly hideous. Don't send me any more such 'buttonholes' to wear with my sack-cloth and ashes.

Before your letter arrived I had written a short obituary article on Toole. I wired to the 'Saturday' to withdraw it; but too late. It is very painful reading in print. Of course, it is 'in the main true' that actors are mortal and must sooner or later go the way of all flesh. But 'it was not for an actor's brother' to have drawn the public's attention to that horrid fact. If only your letter had arrived a day or two earlier!

If you will promise never to refer to this or anything else in my unfortunate and false posistion, I shall be indeed delighted to come to Efford. Will you ask your mother whether I might come on Saturday, 18th? I hope she is very well; and I look forward to meeting your brother — who, I expect, hit on someone better than Kerslake. Have you heard from Pinker?

Yours ever,
Max

Max was already a very great celebrity, and I was rather nervous with him, and never quite knew when he was 'pulling my leg' in his inimitably subtle manner. I was deeply impressed by his elegance and perfect poise — but slightly shocked when he wanted to kiss me!

The next letter from Herbert, which must have been written on the heels of the last, reveals much of him.

August 9   Garrick Club

Your last letter has been sent to me from Marienbad. Here I am back again and am confronted by the furies in the way of worry. When may I come to you? Will you kindly let me know whether it will be convenient to your mother? I hope to get my motor on Monday next. Has Max been with you yet? That was a very amusing little account of me and my supposed helplessness. The last few days of my stay at Marienbad were fraught with adventure of the most acute sort – however I am glad to say that I did what was right and all ends well. No one would believe the story as it happened. When you are a great novelist, I will supply you with a new and original plot. Marienbad is too beautiful – you really ought to go there one year. I came back in the most buoyant health – the cliffs of Dover frowned whitely at me.

All goes well with the rehearsals of 'Winter's Tale' and Viola is a great joy to me. I have really good inspirations for Antony and Cleopatra. I am beginning the play with a vision of the Sphinx in the desert, the stars shining in the dark sky. Slowly the vision vanishes and Antony and Cleopatra are seen sailing in the barge just as it is described by Enobarbus – they land and speak of love. The end of the play is the same as the beginning – passion has raged its brief day – battles have been fought – Antony and Cleopatra are both dead – and Caesar has come and gone in triumph, night has fallen again, and through the darkness we see once more the vision of the calm sphinx – the embodiment of Fate, the eternal stars are still shining indifferent to the fret and strife of human passions. I quite understand your brother's feelings about our people, but you know we are not ignoble entirely, and we have enormous power for good if we only care to exercise it – have we not? With the decline of dogma in religion, our stage will become stronger and stronger. How blind are the bishops!

It always delights me when you write about yourself – that was a splendid touch of femininity when you spoke of the dream in which you saw blood streaming *on the white sating dress* of milady!

I hope you will be glad to get my little letter – give my kindest regards to your mother and believe me always yours in ardent homage,

H.B.T.

Then, just a week later, further hesitancy:

I am terribly sorry that you should be worried, and about me. Are you sure that I ought to come? Indeed, indeed, I understand the feelings of those others who perhaps do not so readily understand me. But if you want

Olivia as a little girl

Hélène (née Gebhardt),
Olivia's mother

General William Truman,
Olivia's father

Herbert Beerbohm Tree

Olivia, at 12, when she first saw
Herbert Beerbohm Tree, as
Bottom (see left), and fell in
love with him.

Tree and Olivia a few years later

Olivia's confidante, Miss Mackay and a facsimile of the letter Olivia sent to her after her grandmother's death

Stafferton Lodge
Maidenhead

March 22nd

Dearest Lady,
How incompatable this dolorous edge is with the wild mad joy at my heart! Never, never have I been so excited about seeing him before. I suppose because it was put off once & all this week I have been ill, yes really ill with excitement. I could not eat. I felt so sick, was always trembling

Inspired by Olivia's Empire-style dress, Max presented her with this drawing and the pen with which it was executed.

me to come, I will, only it must be that your people are in no way opposed to my coming. I know your mother is not – I mean others – it would be placing you in a false position if I did. I would, unless welcome, far rather meet them in London. I am sure your sensitiveness will tell you that I am right in this feeling, however great would be the privilege of seeing you again. You see, here am I who can be of no mundane advantage to you, a young woman who has her fate to make. I used to tell you all this again and again and should not my first consideration be for your *greater* happiness in the future? Think, think of this deeply once more. If you decide that I am to come, I am at your command, but only if there is no chance of any misunderstanding.

So will you please wire me here in the morning or write a letter to reach me before two o'clock tomorrow (Friday). If you think it better for me to postpone the visit let me know, and I will motor to see my children who are at Shaftesbury.

Pray, pray do what is best for yourself – talk to your mother about it. You will, I am sure, understand what *spirit dictates this* and how delightful it would be to me to be with you in your home once more.

My heart's best wishes.   Yours ever sincerely,
                                                                          H.B.T.

Shall I come with Max or alone?

Eventually I think he came accompanied by Max. I have a snapshot of them together, which later appeared in the *Tatler*.

The second visit, when Max joined the party, was necessarily less intensely romantic, but evidently good value. Olivia described it thus in a letter of August 24th written on board the yacht 'Widgeon' in which she was sailing with her brother Billy.

Dearest Aunt Judy,
        I dont know how soon this will reach you as you seemed vague as to your movements – I am so glad you have been so happy in Ireland – is darling Jack [Olivia teased Miss Mackay with frequent references to 'darling Jack' – possibly her employer or son of the family] as devoted as ever?! – I hope you feel much better for the change. Since my last I have been thrilled again by the presence of my dear lord – After all the scene with Billy he was unwilling to come – but I talked – or rather wrote, the latter into reason – he promised to try and like the beloved who, on hearing this on Friday announced his intention of appearing the next day –

All Saturday morning went without a line from him, till at 3 he wired he was motoring and would be there about ½ – I dropped the pen in the middle of a sentence in a criticism I was writing – and flew to robe myself – half past three – a quarter to 4 – a quarter and half past came – and no Herbert – my hair assumed a vertical position whilst I cursed the obstinacy – which made him use a car against my express injunctions – Then I received a telegram from Fareham to say his geography was so involved he couldn't be there before 5. I breathed again – and waited with more or less patience until 5.45 when the precious creature turned up – There was of course much joy at our happy reunion – and we had a long and very satisfactory talk, during which I learned that my worst fear is groundless – He was in the very best of health and spirits tho' abominably fat – and very devoted tho' he had just come on from his lady who is recruiting at Shoreham!! One Col. Enthoven whom you may remember was staying – and Miss Jupp [a family friend] dined – and Max duly turned up. I did not sleep at all that night from excessive love!

Next morning we had a jolly little walk before breakfast – and afterwards we all played crazy croquet – when my dearest – who had never tried before showed a remarkable sense of direction! – can you picture Malvolio – D'Orsay – Herod – Fagin – Caliban   Falstaff – playing that noble game?!! I then took many photographs of him – which if successful I will duly send you – and we lunched when he was more dazzlingly brilliant than I have ever heard him – some of his Irish stories were *inimitable*! About 3 he went off to Shaftesbury where his two children are – and I did not seek to detain him. I think a woman who comes between a man and his children unforgivable – but how lovely for them having *such* a father – so devoted – how characteristic – ladies one and two – and then the kids! Max did his best to console me for the afternoon – a hard task as I was on the verge of tears!

. . . Tuesday we all went out sailing – when Max disappointed us all very much by enjoying himself very much instead of being sick! – Next day he took his departure . . . Thursday I go to Inchmery [the home of Constance, Lady De La Warr, which was nearby] for a week to act in Oscar Wilde's 'Importance of Being Earnest' – which I am very cross over, as it sure to be rotten as Margaret [Lady De La Warr's daughter] has no idea whatever of acting – and has caused me to miss both the Dublin Horse show, and the first night of the 'Winters Tale' to which – and supper afterwards Herbert asked us – I am *so* sick over it! Max has promised to telegraph the next morning, as otherwise I should not know how things went till Monday, which would be dreadful, for after all it is the creation of Herberts brain and his child is acting in it. I don't know my old part a bit –

and don't believe I ever shall! – they are so hard to learn. You have all my news I think – and as I have sprained my thumb writing hurts somewhat – I am very happy – things have settled down so well – in the days when my highest ambition was merely to see my lord off the stage – how little I thought he would ever be our guest! – how wonderful – how exquisite it is! – Write to me – and believe me with every possible wish for your further enjoyment ever thy OMT

Herbert was now going on a provincial tour, and whilst he was absent a friend of my mother's, who was shocked at my passion for him, informed her of some damaging gossip he had heard about him. I am sorry to say that my mother listened, and tried to persuade me to believe it. Of course I was only furious, and wrote and told him what had been said. The following letters show how deeply he was wounded, and I am sure that the one in which he returned to addressing me formally as 'Miss Truman' must have frozen me with horror!

Central Station Hotel, Newcastle-on-Tyne

My dear Miss Truman,
        I will write without fail to-morrow.   Yours sincerely,
                                                                                        H.B.T.

How *could* you listen?!

But before the explanation, Olivia's performance in an amateur production of The Importance of Being Earnest *at Inchmery took place, and on September 6th Max was writing:*

My dear Olivia,
        Many thanks for your delightful account of things. Tonight is *the* night, isn't it? And I have been clapping my hands vigorously, from time to time, throughout the evening, and writing an article – 'At Last An Actress' – for the Saturday Review, and hurling phantom bouquets across imaginary foot-lights, and telepathically asking your mother whether she isn't almost afraid to possess such a daughter. Lady D L W has very kindly asked me to come and stay on the 20th or 26th for a week-end. But on the 20th I go to Italy. Perhaps it is just as well; unless your reports are very much exaggerated! As I expect they are. Has the clergyman offered you his hand in marriage? And is your off-hand tone about him a mask for infatuation? I am going to see the 'Winter's Tale' tomorrow night. I only

went in for the last part of it on the first night – just to see that all was going well. I hope the Inchmery household wasn't hoiked out of bed on Saturday night by the arrival of my telegram? It never occurred to me that it would be despatched before Sunday morning. But probably it wasn't.

Yours ever,
Max

Olivia sends her photographs of Tree to Miss Mackay:

September 16   Efford Park, Lymington

My dearest Aunt Judy,

    I enclose you the promised photos of the precious man – which please mount in rubies and diamonds and fall down before! it would not be the first time you have worked under that inscrutable gaze tho', would it?! – I think they are very good – and tho' not flattering the best I have ever seen of him – the round one *fascinates* me – all his worst qualities – his sansuality – his temper – his conceit – his obstinacy – come out in it – and above all – everything that he has suffered. The one of the group I call *too* funny – we look just like the newly-married coachman and ladies made – I look 'ain't 'e a fine feller' and he looks 'ain't I a dawg to have caught this 'ere young lady'!!!!

Then came further letters from Herbert about the alleged scandal:

September 17   Central Station Hotel, Glasgow

    I am so sorry that I have not been able to write yet, but naturally it is not a light task to write and I am not sure the letter should not be addressed to your mother. I have been terribly driven with work. Yesterday I intended to devote the evening to a letter, but we broke down on the motor and did not reach here till 9.30. So do forgive me.

Ever yours,
H.B.T.

And the next day:

    At last I am going to write to you in regard to your letter of some weeks ago. The matter is so painful that I can hardly bring myself to put my pen to paper about it. Of course I was very angry when I first read your letter and my first impulse was to take a journey to see your mother and unbosom myself to her, but I had many other worries, and so I did not go.

It seems to me hardly delicate to enlarge upon such a theme to you – a 'young person' – so I will be as brief as possible. I am very sorry that your mother should have spoken of me in the manner she has done, but, after all, it is natural that she should guard you against such a person as at the time she believed me to be. But for the *man* who repeated the gossip of a spiteful and somewhat discredited lady without taking the trouble to verify the statements he repeated, I have no words to express my contempt. I listen sometimes to the conversation of these men in clubs and always think them some grades below the man who cheats at cards. I wish I could tell this to your mother's informant. I will content myself by saying that the statements in your letter are false.

I have for many years had a friendship with *a* lady – and I think you know of this – to this lady I have been attached by the strongest ties – you are right in assuming that I have not been guilty of dishonourable conduct and I may tell you that the lady in question said to me not very long ago that she thought I 'could not do a mean thing if I tried'. That of course is only her opinion, but I thought that, coming from this woman, it was the highest compliment that had ever been paid me.

The incident has had consequences tragic alike to her and to me, but I know I should not forfeit your good opinion, which I so deeply prize, if you were acquainted with all that has happened. As you know, it is difficult in life to fulfil one's duties in every relation, but I have striven to be true to what I considered right. I can't say more. As to three 'establishments', I presume my house at Chiswick and my theatre were referred to – I know of no others.

As to yourself, my dear, what better self-respect can I ask than the respect you have given me? You said something rather lax in one letter – but I hope that you will not change from the sweet girl I know you to be. I bless you for all your kindness and helpfulness to and belief in me. I hope you will continue to tell me everything you feel, and do tell your mother that I should be grateful if she would talk to me one day; meantime do not quarrel with any of your people and try to be interested in things other than concern my unhappy self. I wish I could give you the peace of mind I lost in the desert long ago.

Things are going very fairly well both here and in London – you may be interested in the notices which appeared in the papers to-day.

Believe me,   Always yours,

                                                                                          H.B.T.

22 October 1906   Birmingham

How could you think I was offended about the picture in 'The Tatler'? [This refers to a photo of Tree and Max which Olivia had sent to the *Tatler* on her own initiative.] You might send one to the 'Mirror' next week – headed 'Mr Tree's Back again'! I only got your two letters from the Garrick on Friday last and to-night I have your other letter. I have just arrived from London where I went on Saturday night on a sad errand. I have done what is right. Thank you for your many kind words which always give me fresh pleasure and encouragement. I am glad that your people think differently now. Of course we are all liable to these slanders. I think it might be well to ask the person who wrote to you to undo the mischief done as far as possible. But I suppose that is asking too much. I shall myself take occasion to speak to those who are nearest to the utterer of the scandal – not in the way of revenge for I never have that feeling towards women, but by realising the baseness of an action, an elemental decency will sometimes assert itself . . .

No, no, I could not come to you for indeed I am only just in time to save the situation in London, but I am glad to say that things are finishing strongly (it has not been brilliant). I have practically finished all the imaginative work of Antony and Cleopatra, so I shall be able to steam ahead when I get to London, but I shall probably not produce until the 2nd January, – as the time preceding that is a somewhat barren one, theatrically.

Give kindest messages from me to Miss Alexander. Max is still travelling in Italy – and appears to be enjoying himself hugely – life crystallises itself pleasantly for him. I will write again soon.

Ever yours,
H.B.T.

The matter seems thus to have been dropped. There is only one hurried little note that autumn which I spent in London often seeing him.

Wednesday evening

I have been away ever since last night – and am feeling ill and tired. I hope your mother is better – and that you are able to go out and enjoy yourself. Can you not manage to come to see the play to-night? Things are not going well with Richard yet, but I am still hoping.

Yours ever,
H.B.T.

I think it may have been during this time that he faced a domestic crisis. It was perhaps inevitable that I should at least have dallied with the idea of some time marrying Herbert, and I think that one or two clairvoyants, as usual picking up the wishes of one's subconscious, promised that I should do so. There was indeed a time when it came within the bounds of the possible, in so much as his wife met with a very bad car accident which might easily have killed her. As it was, her jaw was smashed, and for the rest of her life she remained with a foolish looking receding chin. As she was out with Lewis Waller, with whom she was having 'an affaire', and Herbert had forbidden her to be seen about with him, the possibility of a divorce arose, and Herbert was dreadfully worried about it all. Personally I think it would have been the sheerest hypocrisy for him, with May and her children in the background, to have brought an action. I know I waited in a car outside the Temple, on one of the occasions on which he was consulting Sir George Lewis, the great divorce lawyer. Ultimately he was counselled to do nothing to create a scandal in his leading position on the stage, at a time when divorce was still regarded fairly seriously. So my matrimonial project receded. In any case, it was an absurd idea, at his age and with his commitments, nor can I imagine a less satisfactory husband. His theatre was his home, and he had no leisure or inclination for anything else. What time he did spend with his family, or families, he must have been tired, and probably irritable, as are all highly strung people when fatigued. Nevertheless his children, more particularly Viola, adored him.

Olivia naturally had a great deal to say about Maud Tree's accident, and the excitement, as always, shows in her spelling.

October 23   Efford Park, Lymington

Dearest Aunt Judy,

I am *indeed* glad to hear that your unfortunate pupil is on the mend . . .

The 'Winters Tale' expedition came off with éclat – Evelyn and I doing a French and American lady in the train – I knowing so little English as to say a succession of awful things to the consternation of the other passengers!! ain't we cracked?! – We lunched at Dieudonné's who did us very well – We then made our state entry into H.M.T. by the private door! – The royal room was uncovered and opened for us – and tea served us there and we were very much en prince! What a contrast – 6 years ago a unknown unit in the dress circle – to-day an honored guest of my lords in the seat of royalty! Little did I think as returning from 'Julius Caesar' I went to bed full of my first love dreams – that to-day I should celebrate the anniversary in the very bed he has slept in – in an atmosphere all whispering of him –

As for the play – well I enclose the critique – The theatre is almost ghastly to me without him – there is a lack of soul, an emptiness that is dreadful – I shuddered to think that some day it must always be so – I had too, a very pungent cause for worry – Mrs Tree was not playing owing to 'indisposistion' – I learnt from my friend Mr Potter [Tree's box-office manager] – that the lady had been thrown out of a motor when out alone with Waller – I was more than disgusted to think that considering it was only at her child's tears that my lord consented to take her back once more only two months ago, and how long the issue hung in the balance, that at once, and his back turned she must needs continue to go about with the man he has forbidden her to associate with – I think she must be a mono-maniac – so little self-controle or sense of decency and right, has she. I was in agony lest Herbert with so great a provocation would do something rash – He who has done so much for the morale of the stage cannot risk a fair name and a life's work by what a spiteful woman might say if aggravated – he cannot divorce her because of Putney – if he separates from her she will take the children to whom he is so devoted, and bring the young ones up with lies to hate his name – and now not less than before, the step would half kill poor Viola – was ever man so tied down – or so remorselessly punished for his sins?!

I was so driven desperate, that Sunday I took the extreme and risky step of writing to Miss Collier and begging her as a trusted friend now near him – to use these arguments – I know what a danger it was but I am *certain* I can trust the woman – and I have never yet been mistaken – and I dared not write straight to him for fear of arousing suspicions that otherwise might not have been his. Imagine my excitement when I saw Monday that he had been to town and seen her – or according to the paper 'satisfied himself of her satisfactory progress'! *How* I burn to know what passed! to-day I have had a letter from him by which I gather he has done nothing rash, but acted with prudence – on receipt of it I threw off the veil and wrote to him begging him to be calm – He has I think stopped further publicity tho' many will doubtless guess – several have asked me already – and I have denied utterly that she was with the Jew – but it makes me *frantic* to know whose name she is so dragging in the mud – that the very employes at the theatre jump to the conclusion who she was with – Mon dieu but the man is a constant anxiety! nevertheless I am only living for the moment when I can cast myself into his arms again after so long a separation – Why could not all our troubles have been ended the other day – by something worse than a cut face? . . .

There is a further letter partly on this subject dated November 4th.

. . . I use 'Mrs Warren' and your sisters address for sending up Herberts photos to papers as then Madame cannot trace them – that is all. A very good one of his and Max's backs, together with a very clever article appeared in the 'Tatler' some weeks back. Constance Collier answered me with a sledge-hammer saying she could not dream of discussing her friends private affairs with a stranger! which only shows how truly she is to be trusted! Nothing, I am thankful to say has happened there beyond his turning her [Maud Tree] out of his theatre – but what he must endure with her puts black murder in my heart! . . .

Two further references occur to meetings with Tree during a winter when Olivia's mother had taken a house in London.

December 2   23, Charles Street, Berkeley Square

. . . I have been to 'Richard' again – always a fresh joy to me – and went and had a nice long talk with Viola who was *so* delightful and *most* gracious. I hear she likes me – but has 'taken me off' to perfection! I am going to the last night – when I hope she will show me! – The night before last Herbert came to supper and was I think nicer to me than he has ever been – which may be accounted for by his being outside a bottle of good champagne – and I don't know when both of us have been so ideally happy – some very worrying affairs that had been making him – and consequently me, quite wretched, had just come right – so it was really delightful – my last vision of him was going out into the moonlight at 2 a.m. with his kit bag under his arm en route for Chiswick! as the butler had gone to bed – one wonders what his thoughts about that bag were!
    . . . To-night we have a dinner at the Savoy with B.P. [Baden Powell] on – (I don't mean he's on!!!!) – Herbert has given me a very beautiful big curb chain bracelet – symbolizing the chain that binds me to him!!! – it is fastened on me and cannot move this side of the fire! . . .

December 12   Efford Park, Lymington

. . . I forgot to say I went to a lecture at H.M.T. when Herbert talked a considerable amount of rot – and then took me out motoring with him – and was so nice that at that point the curtain falls! Saturday I went to Maskelyn & Devants which is really wonderful – some tricks being perfect

miracles of ingenuity – In the evening I went to the last performance of
'Richard' (the 5th time I've seen it!) which as usual I thoroughly enjoyed –
Viola was most gracious – she is *such* a dear. Evelyn brought Norah Boyle a
cousin who stayed at Hamsell with me and who has leanings towards my
preserves – decorating her walls with him ect:! He shook hands with her
which she has not yet got over. Had she done so with God Himself she
could not be more excited! – she wrote and told me she thought him
'tremendously fascinating' – and someone else that he had 'exquisite blue
eyes' – I told Evelyn to tell her to 'keep off the grass' – and she suggests
'standing room only' would be appropriate! – but then you know how
vulgar she is! He must have behaved pretty badly as Miss Boyle enquired
how long he had been in love with me and said anyone could see it with
half an eye! He gave me his rosary en souvenir . . . He is coming here in a
week or ten days – won't it be lovely? – He is very devoted now! . . .

The note he found time to write me on Christmas Day was all I could have
wished.

Christmas Day   His Majesty's Theatre

    I send you all my heart's dearest wishes and ask every blessing for
you and yours. I am looking forward to seeing you on Thursday and will
keep Friday open as you wish. Do pray forgive me for not having written
during these days but I have been throwing myself with all my energy and
every minute of my time into this new venture – up till 6 and 7 for days
running. The work is stupendous, but all will be well, I think. I don't know
how to get through even now, and have to work to-day. I am writing to
your mother. Thanks, dear, for all your kindness, thanks, thanks, thanks,
thanks and again thanks.

                                                    Ever yours,
                                                    Herbert

1907

In January he again promised to visit me, but as usual there were difficulties:

10 January 1907   His Majesty's Theatre

My kindest friend,

      I cannot tell you how disappointed I was that I was unable to get to you last Sunday. I am hoping it may be possible this Sunday – but Viola is all alone in London and I feel that I must do my duty by her. I am sure you will understand. But I will wire you to-morrow. If unable to get away, I will motor down one night next week. I long to have a long talk with you. Viola was discussing you the other day – she thinks you remarkable.

    All goes well here. I have today had my first free day – having motored into the country. It has been a slavish time. I wish you were in London for good. Give my kindest regards to your mother.

Ever yours,
Herbert

January 18

      A thousand thanks for your dear letter – and for your telegram. I shall wire you to-morrow if it is to be this Sunday or next. I am sorely perplexed. If I am able to come on Sunday, it will probably be by motor – for the early train I shall miss – in all probability. But you have given me the choice of two Sundays, have you not?

    You are indeed an angel of kindness.

    I will explain everything to you when I see you.

    I hope you are happy and making others happy – but not too happy.

Ever yours,
H

I have just wired you. I am distressed that I did not get your letter until this evening – for I should have been at my post. And I am very very unhappy to cause you a moment's pain – please forgive me out of your illimitable bounty of forgiveness. I had fully intended coming to you on Sunday and had arranged everything, but frankly Viola is quite alone and I felt it to be my duty to look after her – you are not alone dear, so perhaps you will understand that I did right.

I told you I would come one night, and to-night should have been the night, but something very important has been happening to-day – you will probably read about it in the newspapers to-morrow. The German Emperor has sent me an invitation to go to Berlin and I have to see all sorts of important people to-night and to-morrow morning. Is it not a great coup? You see it is more than a mere personal compliment to me – it has an international aspect and I am sure you will rejoice for me.

On Wednesday I have a Matinee – but I will start on Wednesday night. No, I find there is no train until 6 o'clock in the morning. Wire shall I take that or the 10.15 train? Or shall I go to Southampton? Don't forget to wire or write to-morrow. But do not write angrily – I could not bear that.

I long to have a serious talk with you – I should be much more angry than you were I in your place – you have indeed been forbearing with my fate, for that it is.

I sent you a telegram, I hope it prevented your going to that other station – Brockenhurst, I think. Dear, dear child, do remember there is not only myself to consider, but *yourself* and that is really more important. I had a long thought about you to-day, and Viola spoke to me about you – she has a wonderfully understanding nature.

There are heaps of things I want to tell you of. I am sorry you are not always or oftener in London – but yet – but yet.

If you would prefer that I should not come, let me know. I suppose I could not drive you and your mother back to London – sending the motor down earlier?

Write me a kind little letter, and believe me,

Ever your devoted friend,
Herbert

But from the next undated note, it is obvious that in the end he succeeded.

I can't tell you how disappointed I am that you are not coming up – but I hope it may be soon. Can't you manage to come up with your maid? It was lovely with you the other day, and your mother was infinitely kind and good.

I have my car back now, so perhaps I might fetch you, or meet you half way one day. I am still worried about home affairs but still hopeful that things may be better.

God bless you, dear.

Yours ever,
H

Apart from a hasty note – 'I am rushed off my feet with work and my brain feels like Berlin wool' and a reference to Olivia's new home at Landford Manor, there is no word from Tree until this letter, dated March 20th, in which for the first time he refers to Olivia's devoted maid, Barbara Wiltshire, and the first biography of him, by Mrs George Cran. The 'new little play' was probably The Van Dyck *adapted by Cosmo Gordon from the French of Eugene Fourrier Peringue. 'The Rutland people' are the family of the Duke of Rutland, with whom the Trees were on intimate terms.*

A thousand thanks for your dear letters. It seems ages since I saw you. I will send Mrs Cran's book as soon as possible – you might make some suggestions. If you happen to be able to come to London before the publication, you might meet her.

I am glad all is well with Wiltshire – I don't remember writing to her. I only wrote to you about her – such devotion as hers is to be valued.

The Rutland people wanted me to go there, but I avoided doing so – things are rather sad at home – and pity is a wide bridge.

Our new little play appears to be a real success, and the houses are fuller every night, so I am very hopeful. All goes swimmingly in Berlin. Be very sweet to your mother, won't you dear Olivia. Give her my kindest regards. I may be able to come early next week – as I am closing the theatre on Wednesday, Thursday and Friday – but of course the Berlin rehearsals tax one. I hope to be able to write you another note to-morrow.

Ever your servant,
Herbert

One day about then Herbert slipped up in the dome, and in falling bent a rib on a chair; this more or less laid him up, and I was in a distracted state, being unable to see him, when naturally to have nursed him would have been heaven to me. I went to interview his doctor, and hung round the theatre for the latest news. As a souvenir I have the X-ray photograph of the injured rib.

His Majesty's Theatre

I am in bed – so am afraid you cannot see me – I acted in agony last night but went out to supper – made a speech and returned at 4 a.m. I shan't get up till 1.

I am so sorry to miss you – I suppose if your Aunt were with you, you might say a kind word through a curtain.

His Majesty's Theatre

I have had an excellent night and the pain is much less this morning. I feel I am mending quickly – please don't worry, dear – it is natural that these things should take a little time.

I could not come to Waterloo, as I must stay in bed until the perform-ance. If you will leave me your address, I will wire you to-day. I think it would be better not to come here.

Thursday

Since writing you last, I have again been suffering – this business has been most obstinate, and I suppose I am a bad patient, having suffered so little hitherto. However, this evening I feel more energy. When are you coming to London again – do let me know. I hope your maid will stay with you, she is evidently devoted to you, and that is a rare blessing. When I see her I will tell her she must not leave you . . .

Write me to the Garrick Club, as they often open letters here. Bless you, bless you, bless you!

Yours,
H

This seems to have been followed by some slight illness of my own.

Your dear letters gave me the greatest joy, but sorrow too in knowing you were ill. I hope all traces have vanished now and that you are already wandering about your garden – beautifying it by your wandering!

I should have written you ages ago, but I have been terribly rushed with work. All goes well now, and I think the play is going to be a big success. I want it, for we have been having a lean time indeed.

I am sending you the book. I am glad to see Mrs Cran has rectified one or two slight betises – generally speaking it is good. I shall come to you as soon as I can – if your kind mother will ask me. I do hope I shall have leisure this season. Are you coming up for the first night of 'A Woman'? Let me know.

I must rush away at this moment when I had promised myself the indulgence of communing with you. I send you my most affectionate greetings.

Yours ever,
H

Previous to this my mother had decided to leave Efford Park which was far more costly than we could ever have afforded. After a little hunting we found a beautiful old house on the other side of the New Forest, off the road from Lyndhurst to Salisbury. It had been a Jacobean farm, restored in the reign of Queen Anne. The interior of the house was charming with three sitting-rooms and about ten bedrooms, and Mother fell for it instantly. The decision was as ill-judged as her previous moves. No longer having to consider my father, she should at last have tried to pay off her debts and in addition taken me to some place where I could meet young people. It did not take us long to discover that it was an isolated and socially dreary spot. The neighbours were of the dullest type, and unfortunately included the family into which I eventually married.

Olivia describes a visit to His Majesty's while Tree was still suffering from his injured rib.

February 23   Landford Manor, Salisbury

Dearest Aunt Judy,

Thanks so much for your most fruity and appropriate cartoon – the likeness is almost overpowering!! So glad you enjoyed yourself the other day, and loved the dimmed illusive one – dimmed illusive ones generally are fascinating! [Probably a reference to the 'demmed elusive Pimpernel' in *The Scarlet Pimpernel* which they had seen together.] After you left I went to H.M.T. and found Herbert was not acting that night – so I sent up notes beseeching him to see more doctors and have hot fomentations, and arranging to come to him late with my cousin. I went off with misery in my heart to 'You Never can Tell' which fascinated me more than ever, and where I got a note putting me off, and saying he was better. Next morning I heard the famous Page Roberts preach about the devil, which bored me knowing him as well as I do! – and in the afternoon went to listen to my divine boys voice at the Oratory – which positively made me sob with emotion! thus doubly fortified I went off to Herbert – I found him better, but cross and worried by people . . . finally 'Anthony' – Everyone – but particularly Constance Collier has improved since the first night – Herbert was in too great pain for me to be able to tell – it was terrible to me to see him, but he was awfully plucky – I had a long talk with Miss Collier, who has quite got over my letter to her, and is very charming and sympathetic – a strong and nice woman. We had supper with him – he looking too odd with his head as ever – and Anthony's understandings! He was in real agony tho' which made me positively sick . . . Herbert is better to-day but was bad yesterday – it is not dangerous but a long job poor darling.

Always Mackay,
Thy
OMT

Tree pays his first visit to Landford, and there is further reference to Mrs Cran's biography.

Good Friday, March 29th 1907   Landford Manor, Salisbury

My dearest Aunt Judy,

      Well, ma chère, my whole weeks news is put into two words – Herberts been! – I think his upper story is unusually bad – first he talked of Sunday then of Monday, and when I enquired how the latter was possible – he wired he had forgotten he had to act!! – have you ever heard the equal of that?! ultimately he fixed on Wednesday – and after the usual muddles and vagueness which attend his movements, he arrived at Salisbury at 8 – and I fetched him out in the car – a raptuous romantic drive in the brilliant moonlight! He *raved* over the house and was most happy – just as passionate and naughty as he could be – and finally – was conveyed back to Winchester by 11 – another divine run. He brought the proofs of the biography of him just coming out, with him – and I sat up nearly all night correcting and reading them. It is only 35 pages – and certainly interesting and clever. He read us the first act of 'A Woman of no Importance' (Oscar Wilde) which he contemplates reviving – quite too beautifully – a very smart phrase is 'A woman who has been married 20 years is like a ruin – one who has been married 4 times is like a public building!!' – another smart 'mot' by the authoress of his book – he told her how Napoleon calling on George Sand was told she was in her bath, and saying 'genius has no sex' walked in – Mrs Cran said 'After all sex *is* only a matter of form'!! – good eh? . . .

The rest of the letter is in a mood of repentance for her conduct, which must have evoked something in the nature of 'I told you so' from Miss Mackay.

April 4

. . . but I think you are under a misapprehension with regard to what I told you in my last – You think that I have had 'to take a pull' – because if I did not disaster would occur – it is not so – I never have been more confident of myself – more capable of managing him than at present – it is just that very capacity for going to a certain length and no further, that being a man, I cannot instil into Herbert – he must either not touche me or lose himself in passion – I can rest in his arms his lips on mine, and be contented – ask for no more – indeed shrink from more – for at such moments I only stand outside myself – and watch myself and him, and am disgusted – at best I only refuse to think, and submit – It is only now tho' that I have awoke to its real wrongness – and because I know too that I must qualify, before my happiness can be given me – I must sacrifice the moments of rapture in his arms – What other women have to give up for their safety I give up for a scruple – for it is nothing else, seest thou, my lady – and make thyself easy that I am in no danger . . .

Herbert did not forget her birthday on April 11th:

. . . Herbert wired to me, late at night, so I got it first thing Thursday morning – wasn't it darling of him to remember?! – and sent me the most glorious box full of flowers from Gerards – roses, lilies and lilac!! – I have been revelling in a bower of sweetness – but now they are dying which wrings my heart!

. . . Of course I am in the 101st heaven over Berlin! – it is really too *divine*! *What* I would have given to be there!! And how his wife must suffer, left at home instead of queening it by his side in this great moment of his life! I wired him 'Allez vaincre: – votre génie l'epée – mes souhaits ardents votre gage'!! – is that not worthy of me?!! – and I sent him off with 'God and thy good cause fight upon thy side – ich bin mit ihn'!! don't you mind me! – truly tho' I am more proud and thankful than I can say . . . and Tuesday we are going over to Bournemouth – Wednesday I go to Portsmouth to see Stella [her friend Stella Buchanan] – and Monday I am for town and the arms of the beloved! . . .

June 1

. . . I then went to Herbert – he being of course late – I sat and watched a rehearsal of the charity matinee to take place there next week – which amused me very much! When he at length turned up, we went and made love in the dome! – mercifully he was very calm! – He looked ill and worried – and had had toothache – and at five I drove him to his dentist – and left him – just having time to catch the train home. To-day I feel rather piano as it was the first time since my illness. I have had a long day. It appears the day before, Cockie Alexander, who has met Felicite at her classes [Felicity Tree, Herbert's second daughter] – went to tea after the performance, with the whole crew in the dome!!! – ma, pa – Viola, and Marjorie Manners [eldest daughter of the 8th Duke of Rutland]! and if you will have it – they brought me up – a curious collection to have my name on their lips!!! – I hear Viola loves making alliterations on my name, such as 'Truman's tricks' or 'Truman on the track'!!! – not so dusty eh?! I have just had a particularly sweet letter from the same young lady – I *am* so thankful she likes me! . . .

July 25

. . . On Sunday we had just gone into the drawingroom after lunch, when the footman (*not* the hall boy!) announced 'Mr Tree'!!! Believing him in Marienbad we thought the lad had gone off it, but sure enough it was my eccentric lord, who had entered by the back door – as the front was not opened quick enough!! I controlled my feelings as best I could, and learned he had been staying the night before at Southampton with Putney and the boy – which I call *quite* disgusting – and was on his way back to town – with the lady at the bottom of the hill! He had a drink – kissed me – and bolted!!!! – It makes a change from my driving him to her, for her to drive him to me – but I hardly think he would have been received back with aplomb if she had known who he'd seen and what he'd done!! – I believe he really did leave England on Tuesday –

Marienbad was always fruitful in the correspondence line, and two letters written in that place came to delight my soul.

2 August 1907   Marienbad

My dear, kind friend,
        A thousand thanks for your sweet letter.
    How you would love being here and how I would love you to be! I am delighted about your novel – what an excitement! – you ought to get Max or some equivalent (if there is one) to look through your proofs. Naughty Max has a novel in his pigeon-hole but carefully abstains from publishing it

– females rush in where mere males fear to tread. What fun reciting in the cricket pavilion – it was very brave and fine of you to do it – and the result justified your valour.

You are too too good to me, dear – when you should be thinking of all your future – I often ask myself if it is not selfish that I should allow you to be so prodigal to me who am so torn and so battered. But some day the ideal man will come along – and then all my wealth will be his, for it is yours – I have only held it in trust and it is accumulating with compound interest.

There are not many interesting people here. Miss Mabel Lowther is nice, and Lady Parker, and there are some Americans who attacked me with confetti on the promenade one night, – but there is nobody enthralling, or even beckoning. A man named Charles Boyd (whom you met) is here also – but I am living alone on a beautiful hill overlooking a lovely landscape, and I work up here a great deal. So far 'The Vagabond' and 'Faust' have had my attention, and I am glad to say I can concentrate my mind with great energy, only when worries and misgivings and waking nightmares come do my thoughts go 'on strike'. I shall try to write you a letter from the woods. I wish we could have persuaded your mother to come here – you might tell her it would have been a good 'cure' for you, for you would have seen me so much that you would have become tired of me.

Do write again if you are in the mood. I must dash this moment – but will write again.

Now and always your servant,
Herbert

12 August 1907   Marienbad

I read your charming criticism of the Beloved Vagabond to Locke [W. J. Locke, the play's author] who was delighted – he is here with me. I shall send you the play on my return – I think you will be satisfied.

I am coming towards the end of my 'cure' and hope to see you soon. I have gained several years of youth during my stay . . .

I am a little unhappy as I have not had news from the quarter I wanted but many people there are who love to torture – it is their conception of love. The King comes here on Friday – I don't know whether to wait or to fly.

There are some nice-ish English people here – but nobody enthralling. I am spending my morning writing letters – mostly sad ones . . .

Bless you, sweet soul.

Your devoted,
H

My debut among our neighbours was not made any easier by the appearance of this novel which I had begun at sixteen, called *The Spirit Juggler*. Though less lurid than its predecessors, it was not quite the sort of thing a really nice Edwardian young lady should have written. It dealt with a Ruritanian king and an actor manager who change places, and also wives. It did not take a great deal of perspicacity to note the resemblance of the actor to the proprietor of His Majesty's Theatre, especially as it was dedicated to 'H.T.' – which happened also to be my mother's initials. Besides prejudicing me socially, which Mother should at least have had the sense to prevent by insisting on a *nom de plume*, it was disastrous financially, as the publisher went bankrupt shortly after its publication, leaving half the edition unbound. This was a pity because it got some surprisingly good notices: the dramatic author, Harwood 'I think it is very well written – especially the descriptive parts, and the characters, which I take it are drawn from life.' He was quite right – the lady who eventually finds herself the wife of the actor manager is Miss Olivia Truman as seen through very rose tinted spectacles.

Once more September saw Tree doing the treadmill of a tour, but he yet found time amid his journeys, performances and rehearsals to write and telegraph to me, and to show a vivid interest in the book I had just published.

21 September 1907   Adelphi Hotel, Liverpool

A million thanks for your sweet letter.

I hope Max behaved very gallantly – I am sure he was very happy; while his toiling brother has to eke out an existence in Northern blasts, he is basking in a double sunshine.

I hope the book will be quite satisfactory – *I wish you would send me the proofs!*

All goes well – 'The Vagabond' comes out wonderfully at rehearsal – it seems all smooth sailing, so I have the greatest hopes – but one never knows if there is a flaw in the bell, to make its music mute. Viola is with me and is very sweet – poor darling she has a sore throat to-day and I am a little anxious about her . . .

Do write me – while I am here, my best address is c/o The Conservative Club. Your letters are always a joy and an excitement to me.

Ever your devoted,

H

⬛ *1907* ⬛

October 4   Shelbourne Hotel, Dublin

My dear,

    I am so ashamed but I have been absolutely rushed with work so that I have been tired out, and have to write every day about some worrying affairs. But we are nearing the end of our labours. The Vagabond is going splendidly, I think.

    Do write to me as often as you can – your letters are always a joy and a consolation.

    You seem to be very gay – but don't forget me quite. I must come to you as soon as I get back. Anxieties are heaped upon anxieties during this tour. I am asking Miss Leverton to send you the newspapers regularly so that in future you will know all about us.

    The people treat us splendidly here. I feel I am an Irishman while I am in Dublin. Why can't you manage to come?

    I must try to write to you every few days to make up for my remissness. I'll write a really nice letter, but now I have to eat something (6 o'clock). I have had nothing all day – so forgive my intellectual emptiness – in sympathy with my other.

Ever yours,

H

⬛

Among the near neighbours attending the particularly ugly Victorian church in Landford were the Wigrams from Northlands. She was a widow with three daughters and three sons, two daughters and one son being married. The eldest son was a giant, an amiable but quite unintelligent person, married to a South African; the second was in the Navy, hearty, boozing, kindly; the third son and youngest child had been in the Somersets and was seconded to a post in Nigeria.

    Shortly after our going to Landford he came home on leave. He had been seriously ill in Africa, and one Sunday accompanied his mother to church. Their pew was just behind ours, so that he had ample opportunity for making a thorough inspection of me. The result was so entirely favourable that before long he was spending most of his time with us, not with the approval of his family who, I have only lately gathered, took part in discussions behind closed doors of the undesirability of the new young person at the Manor. Their concern was further increased when he announced his intention of not returning to his post, but coming out of the army, and starting a garage, with the unconcealed intention of remaining near me. This decision was unfortunate for both him and me. He was a very good-looking young man, with

79

wavy brown hair very similar to my own, and hazel eyes of exceptional brilliance. He was extremely quick in the uptake, with a very witty and original turn of phrase. His mother had called him her Benjamin, adored and spoiled him, with the result that he was quite undisciplined. He fell very violently in love with me, and I did nothing to discourage him. After all, to be loved is always flattering, and I was in a way very lonely, and thankful for some young companionship. I found what the Americans so inelegantly term 'necking' an amusing occupation, if distinctly unfair to him. It in no way affected my adoration of Herbert, but as I was well aware he was still increasing his family on the left, I saw no disloyalty to him in indulging in a little gallantry. I made no secret of it to Herbert, and indeed seem to have appealed to him to find Cyril some sort of job – I cannot imagine what, since he had no qualifications beyond those connected with soldiering, and a natural flair for the interiors of motor cars. Herbert responded with his usual kindness.

October 14   Central Station Hotel, Glasgow

Here we are, having 'moved on' from Dublin. On the journey hither a clever young lady (a friend of Viola's) read your book or parts of it and pointed out various passages to me – she told me she considered the book really able. I read two chapters but felt 'shy' of devouring it all – do you understand that feeling? It is like looking at oneself in a flattering glass. The book is delightfully got up – I wonder what the critics will say! My dear, I am afraid there are certain almost personal references which will be taken notice of. I am so glad you have dedicated it to your mother! Now as to your last letter, I will do all I can. What do you want me to do – take him into the theatre? – Is he clever? – And in what way? – engineering you say or motoring – Do you mean as electrician in the theatre or as gentleman-driver? . . .

You must keep this matter of your friend before me. Shall he come to see me? or do you prefer to wait till I come up from Manchester in three weeks' time? Do write to me as often as you can, and remember your sweet determination not to flirt with any of your many adorers.

I thought of you on the first night of the Vagabond. I wired you to-day about the book. A man who read it told me he thought it brilliant. I wonder what Max thinks? I will try to write to you more fully to-morrow. All promises well here.

Your devoted,
H

This next letter, sent from Glasgow on October 24th, was written on paper headed 'Mr Tree and His Majesty's Theatre Company'.

We have been rehearsing Edwin Drood every day – it really promises well, though it is of course a sheer melodrama. It has been raining incessantly during the last fortnight, and a wet pall has been hanging over the City. I can imagine people going mad under it.

Viola has been very sweet and looks after me like a mother – she says I am eleven years old!

I have nothing for you but a record of work – so I will ask you all about yourself – how is the book going? Do write and tell me all about it – and your new one – is it progressing?

Thus far I had written when I sent you the telegram on a motor journey to Edinburgh from Dumfries where we had been staying from Saturday till Monday – a most lovely drive – a charming lady was with me, but I wish it had been you! Ever since then, I have been trying to sit down to write, but the world and the devil have been 'at' me all the time – so I snatch these few minutes before leaving for the theatre.

To-morrow I will sit down and give you a real account of all that is going on. To-night during the entractes I have to finish a story for a magazine!

All goes well. I won't forget your friend – so tell him.

Good night. God bless you always.

Yours,
H

October 30

I wrote yesterday and promised to write again to-day. We rehearsed from 11.30 till 3.30 and made good progress. I think Edwin Drood promises very well. In regard to your new friend, I hope you won't think me intrusive if I beg you to take care – of course he may be the ideal man – but on the other hand he may not. I think it beautiful of you to have this 'mothering' instinct – this quality is the surest sign of a great womanly nature – but sometimes our finest impulses lead us astray and make us clothe casual objects with lovely garments of our own weaving. Thank you for what you say about home affairs. I am having her to stay at Manchester next week and have allowed Viola to go up to London when she was free – so you see I am not unmindful of being kind. Indeed I hope I always remember such things. Please write to me as you can spare time. I think I told you I will make every effort to further your friend's interests, but *be careful of yourself!* – and do tell me *everything* – perhaps you have not told me.

Ever yours,
H

There is unfortunately a gap in Olivia's own letters to her confidante from October 1907 to October 1909, a loss which Olivia herself lamented later on. Meanwhile Tree's tour continued almost to the end of the year.

November 13   The Queen's Hotel, Manchester, Ltd

Thanks again for your sweet letter – no of course I was not angry – you must introduce me to him as soon as possible – I shall be most anxious to serve him in order to serve you.

Yes, the Manchester critic is a terror – I had called him 'anaemic' last year and they are hitting back. Write a little note to the Editor – that does good – but they must have been *bombarded*. I shall deal with them before I leave Manchester. But everyone who comes here says the same about the paper.

I am delighted to hear the book is being well reviewed. All goes well with Drood – can't you manage to come to Birmingham if I arrange it? Seats went to your old nurse.

Bless you, dear sweet girl. I am beginning to get home-sick. I don't mind about Hare [John Hare the actor who had been knighted] – he has done very well – and of course I have many enemies. One must expect injustice and heartaches if one does not stoop to 'play the game' – but at least one has one's own panache!

Give my love to your mother and keep sweet and good.

Believe me ever, Your friend,
Herbert

December 7   Central Station Hotel, Newcastle-on-Tyne

I wrote you a few lines yesterday. I am getting quite London-sick. How is all with you? – Do write me to Birmingham and tell me. I am to lunch with Marie Corelli – shall I ask her to read your book?

Max is still abroad. What a happy life he has! Mine is not a very happy one just now.

82

I shall go up to London to-night and shall not arrive in Birmingham till the evening – and that is our last week. At Christmas I hope to go to Paris to see Sardou who wants to do a play for me. [Victorien Sardou was a popular French playwright.]

I must send you Faust which is, I think, destined to be a great success. Viola arrived last night and returns with me to-night. I hope you'll like the little fairy-tale – it is rather hastily written but the idea is right, I think.

I hope you are taking great care of yourself, dear.

Good-bye, I am very dull and numb to-day – and I am only writing in order to keep my promise. I feel unfit for communion.

Ever yours,

H

December 24   His Majesty's Theatre, London

My dear sweet friend,

I am sending you some little gifts with every good wish. May I come to see you next week and make myself very happy? Or do the spirits* forbid?

What a lovely gift you sent me – much too fine for me!

I have had a pretty terrible day – but I am free now – I'll tell you when I see you.

I send you with what is left of me all good wishes and to all the people you love – you sweet woman! I had intended devoting myself to a long letter to you – but these two days I have not had a moment when I was not on the rack.

Nothing for *you* to worry about – it is over now.

Ever your devoted,

H

* A dig at my interest in spiritualism [Olivia's note].

1908 and 1909

After his Christmas greetings follow four hurriedly written notes making appointments, and they prove that I was seeing him fairly regularly. In fact from then on* I really entered into my own. I could go to the theatre whenever I wished by merely telephoning the box office. I generally had the royal box, and the dear little room behind it, always nicely arranged with flowers, coffee and drinks, and there between the acts and after the play he would join me. The clang of the iron door to the stage, and then the quick light steps heralded his approach – the smell of grease-paint now makes me very sad. He would take me with him to what he called 'see me eat', or issue the command 'drive with me'.

Sometimes I went with him to other theatres; on one occasion I sat with him and Granville Barker at Galsworthy's play *Justice*. I used also to go to suppers at the Carlton. One when Sir Thomas Beecham was present was specially amusing. Speaking of whom, Herbert made one of his quickest sorties. The celebrated conductor had rented His Majesty's for a season, and was putting on an opera with a Scottish theme, to advertise which he engaged a piper to perambulate through the streets. When Herbert heard of this he was shocked, for vulgarity in advertisement he disliked. 'Ah Beecham,' he said, 'I see that the pills are beginning to work!'

All this time my life continued to revolve entirely round Herbert; I had no thought or interest apart from him. His plays and all pertaining thereto absorbed me. I think my anxiety as to the success of his first nights exceeded his own. If anything prevented my being present, I made his box-office manager, Mr Potter, a nice and devoted man, send me a telegram to arrive first thing in the morning, and during the actual time of the performance I would remain shut up alone, sometimes in the church which adjoined our garden. I subscribed to a newspaper agency so that every press notice of him came to me, and was stuck into albums. Adverse criticism of him from others

* Olivia was now twenty years old.

85

I could not bear, and to anyone who spoke ill of him I took instant dislike, but I myself used often to find fault, and he stood from me more of this than from anyone else, knowing that my criticism was based on love which only sought his greater glory.

On one occasion Mr Potter told me that after the production of a new play he said to him 'Miss Truman is very pleased with it', to which Herbert replied 'She is a very severe critic, but that is what makes her judgement so valuable.'

My ambition for him was boundless, and I was bitterly jealous of Irving in that many people rated him above Tree – personally I still think without reason. Herbert lived absolutely for his work, and everything he was he expressed through it. His gift of subtle psychology – the tenderness of his heart which made all suffering dreadful to him, his rare sense of humour and wit, his idealism, always striving after the beautiful and the good, his artistic love of colour, sound and form, were all revealed in the theatre. He was not a man so much as an embodiment. His knowledge of the right thing was intuitive – it came in the flashes only vouchsafed to genius. His personality had the dynamic power which can galvanise the dead into life. His energy was amazing: week after week and year after year he would never miss a performance, and in addition was generally rehearsing a new play all day. Times like his Shakespeare festivals, when he would put on a different play each night, meant labour past belief – and all for sheer love of his art. Money meant nothing to him, he spent it like a prince, even though half the time he was on the verge of bankruptcy. He entertained lavishly, for all the artistic notabilities of Europe who came to London went to see him. He was the focal point of the dramatic profession. There is no equivalent to him today, no actor with a reputation for an unbroken series of noble plays, whose name is familiar in remote country cottages.

In July he wrote from Harrogate:

July 18   Tower House, York Road, Harrogate

My dear, dear friend,

Here I am! I have taken a house for a fortnight, so as to be absolutely quiet and to concentrate myself on 'Faust'. I find, by the way, that it wants some editing. I am also taking the 'cure'. I could not get away to Marienbad owing to my harassing affairs, but I think daylight is coming through the clouds that threatened. Thank you for your sweet encouragement, and your good advice.

I am taking great care of my health and return to London on the 1st August. The doctor says I am stronger than I was five years ago – and indeed I think I am . . .

How is your mother? And how is your brother? I am quite alone here, with two servants – rather original, is it not? But I feel my isolation is necessary – to *mental* isolation I am used.

I wish you were here! I intended writing to you yesterday but have been busy moving from my Hotel.

I send you as many pretty thoughts as there are daisies on the lawn. By the by, I must tell you what Iris [Iris Tree, his youngest daughter] said to me the other Sunday. I took her into the garden and told her I wanted to talk to her very seriously. I had heard that she no longer believed in fairies (we were sitting on the lawn) – she felt awkward between hurting my feelings and not telling the truth. Then she said: 'Daddy, I believe in fairies when I see them, but I haven't seen any just lately. They say there is a fairy in each of these daisies – I don't see any but, Daddy, each of these daisies is a fairy to me.'!

Ever your grateful friend,
H

Tuesday   His Majesty's Theatre

I am grieved, my dear, that you should have been offended with me for not sending you a telegram, but if I promised to send you one it went out of my mind. It was sweet of you to care. I hope I am forgiven or that you will forgive me on Sunday, when I hope to see you, if (after my bad conduct) you will allow me to come.

All went well on Saturday night at 11.45 – I went to Netley House [Sir Alfred Fripp's nursing home in Henrietta Street] and submitted to ether and other terrible inflictions – I think I must have fought like a tiger – however the operation was successful and I only suffered from the effects of sickness – pretty badly, though, and nearly lost my voice.

On Monday night I acted and now my eye is completely beautiful! So that is the tragical history of last Sunday and Monday.

Fripp is indeed a treasure. All goes well here. Can I do anything for you before Sunday?

Of course, if you don't want to see me (I think Viola wants to come too), you have only to command my absence! –

With affectionate homage,   I am yours,
H.B.T.

The letter refers to an operation on his eye which of course filled me with solicitude. He came to stay with us just afterwards accompanied by his daughter. There seems to have been no Marienbad that year, but instead he joined his family in France.

August 15   His Majesty's Theatre

I am just off – I think to stay at or near Boulogne for a few days – that is till Monday. How I wish we could meet! I hope the rest of your trip turned out brightly.

All goes well with the Faust rehearsals – I think it will be quite wonderful. You must come and see some of the rehearsals.

Please give my kindest regards to your mother. I must be allowed to keep my promise to pay you a visit before the 5th September.

It is rather pleasant in London just now with glorious weather and the sense of being (socially) on a desert island.

Ever your devoted friend,
H

A letter of October 15th, also sent from His Majesty's Theatre, indicates that there had been another visit to us after his return from the continent.

My dear friend,

I have been constantly intending to write to you since our visit, but have had a baddish time – lost my voice and have got through the nights with difficulty, and during the days I have been kept here in 'durance vile' – I find the responsibilities of management bearing hard upon me – to-day I hope to get into the air for an hour or two. It was a delightful visit that Viola and I had – do thank your mother for her great kindness to us – but I believe Viola has written to her. I am sure you will miss your brother – it is pleasant to know of such deep devotion on both sides. Please wish him all good luck and good health from me. I daresay you might go to India for a visit. We had a capital drive up to London, with never a break-down.

Faust goes well, but is no longer quite so brilliant – however I hope we are safe till Christmas. When am I to see you again? Your mother talked of coming up at the end of the month?

I am feeling a little melancholy to-day – so you have a companion in your sadness.

Au revoir soon,

Ever yours,
H.B.T.

If the Mackay letters of this period had not been lost they might have explained an unusually long break in the Olivia/Tree correspondence here. As it is, Olivia takes up the story in the spring of the following year:

My twenty-first birthday* coincided with Herbert's marvellous all-star production of *The School for Scandal* – the greatest collection of well known names that has ever been got together. Herbert himself of course played Sir Peter very successfully to the Lady Teazle of Marie Löhr. The first appearance of Godfrey Tearle was as a powdered footman who brought on an interval notice. Herbert marked the twin occasions of this great evening and my birthday by giving a huge supper party in the banqueting hall of the dome. It was a brilliant scene attended by a number of the best known men and women of the artistic world. Herbert had asked me whom I would like invited as my special guest, and I opted for John Galsworthy, whose books I admired greatly. I found him a delightful personality, and we had a long discussion on survival, in which he did not believe. So interested were we that I doubt if either of us paid much attention to the quail and oyster pudding – Herbert's hospitality was always lavish. Galsworthy expressed some astonishment at his invitation, as he knew Herbert very slightly, and rarely went out to supper. It was with pride that I claimed responsibility for his presence!

13 April 1909

My dear Olivia,

I was only able to send you my good wishes by telegram on Sunday. I had indeed hoped to be with you, but I could not get away. I had to give a decision on a very important point – Hall Caine's play, which I find is too dangerous (politically) to produce at this time – and discussion took up the greater part of the day. [It is not clear what play Tree is referring to here. He never did produce it.]

I hope you had a sweet, peaceful day – of course it was Spring, and that you may always have the Spring in your soul.

I am sending you a little gift. It was lovely having you with us that night – I was afraid to propose your health in my speech.

All goes well with 'The School for Scandal' – I think it really is going to draw for some months – what a relief that will be to me.

Give my kindest regards to your mother.

How are your love affairs getting on?

When are you coming to town again?

---

* Olivia's birthday was on April 11th.

We have a little house at Rottingdean now and Viola and the children are there.

God bless you, dear, during all the years to come.

Ever yours,
Herbert

Is there in it, perhaps, the first suggestion of his becoming background music rather than the main theme? 'How are your love affairs?' he asks, as if he himself was not the only one which still mattered. The plural was indeed applicable to my coquetries!

At the beginning of 1909 I went out to Switzerland to join friends of my brother's at Les Avants above Montreux. It was my first experience of winter sports. I found everything new and exciting and set about learning to ski. My friends soon introduced me to a brother and sister, Oliver and Beatrice Valpy, a really delightful couple with whom I struck up a warm friendship. Oliver had probably the nicest character of any man I ever met — warm and unselfish and intrinsically good. He was tall and angular, by no means handsome, but that made little difference. His sister had a long, very aristocratic face and nose with very clear blue serene eyes and soft fair hair. She was well read, and very interested in opera and the theatre, and for years remained my chief crony.

Also in the hotel was a large red-faced old lady, an ex-mayoress and widow of a knight. For some reason I cannot explain, Oliver and I thought it would be a joke to pretend to her that we were engaged. There must have been some point in it which escapes me, as I can now see none at all. However, the upshot was that we found it a good idea, and decided to take it seriously. Actually it was quite unpardonably stupid, not to say immoral, to contemplate marriage with one man when I was in love with another, but so spoilt and self-centred was I that I saw nothing against this arrangement at all. The extraordinary thing is that Oliver should have kept it up as he was very soon able to see for himself what was going on. Herbert was engaged on the production of Brieux's play *False Gods*. Its Egyptian setting caused him to pay a flying visit to Cairo, and on his way back he stopped at Montreux to visit me. My ecstatic happiness knew no bounds when the great actor manager descended from the train, and later drove with me in a sleigh over the sparkling white roads, the mountains rising above us silhouetted against the blue sky. To celebrate his presence I gave a dinner party at the hotel with a very special menu, to which I invited my friends, including of course Oliver Valpy. He must indeed have been unobservant if he did not notice the open adoration with which I regarded Herbert. The latter only remained one night, and sadly I had to see him depart on his way.

48, UPPER BERKELEY STREET, W.

A letter from Max

The snapshot of Tree and his half-brother, Max Beerbohm, that was sent by Olivia to the Tatler.

Drawing of Tree by John Sargent

Tree as Svengali – one of his most successful rôles

Room in the dome of His Majesty's Theatre showing the alcove study in which Tree and Olivia often met and where he wrote many of his letters to her.

Harry Uniacke, Tree's only serious
rival for Olivia's affections

Cyril Wigram, Olivia's husband

Etta Niven: a close friend of Olivia's
and mother of David Niven

Viola Tree, Herbert's oldest daughter,
who became Olivia's friend

Barring two notes it was not until Herbert went to
another letter from him, received as I was about to sta
mother and sister at Dawlish in Devon, where they ha
delightful visit as their thatched cottage was a little dre
and honeysuckle – Oliver was a keen and clever garde
Herbert evidently returned, and so blind was I to any
of view that I even persuaded the unfortunate Oliver
very fine sweetpeas he grew and send them to His M:

The letter referred to above, from his beloved
Herbert's recently conferred knighthood, which I h:

August 3

At last, I am writing to you to thank you f
not think it is not always a joy to receive them. I a
in the world – taking a pen in my hand gives me
But soon, I shall see you, I hope in your own hom
by word of mouth what the written word tells
hate to hurt you – I should indeed be ungrateful
lives are so far apart, and lately I have been hustl
so the pillar-post has been neglected! How are

So you are going to Oliver – now, don't be s
he seems to be, don't dally with him! Happine
men are so scarce.

I shall be leaving here next Friday; then to
then to London. I should like to postpone the
This time here has done me great good alread
for the fight.

Whatever one does, or whatever one does
Now as to what you say about this Knighth
about *all* these things, and I am probably – b;
whom the distinction has made the least i
was necessary that I should accept it. *You*
chicanery to which a person in my position
renders my enemies innocuous. But I must
that the occasion should have brought me
generous friends I have, who regard this
delight – and this has deeply touched me
world at large. I remain myself just the sa
many know worth only by its label. Th
'Knighted and unashamed'! Believe m

feel
and
you
are
a vi
the
mor
woul
I a
but i
havi
W
I do n
Herbert
previou
knighth
distincti
The i
soon aft
affection
person, I
the quasi
Nor can I
Fonmon
Whate
tremendo
and playi
and the dr
as is evide
she had a
difference
Gentlema
not very ta

ing that I am belittled. I hope that it will cause no shrinkage in my soul,
from the point of view of worldly prosperity, it should help me. And
know I cannot afford to throw that help away – for my responsibilities
great. Now, try to think of it as a blessing and not a curse. It is, after all
tory – a victory coveted and striven for in other quarters. I have still
quiet regard and the deeper understanding of my *friends* – and none
kind and dear than you! Could you see all the letters I have had, you
d not regret it (you shall see the book).
m delighted with Brieux' great play. It will make a deep impression –
may be too profound for the many. Even if it be, I shall be proud of
g given it.
th every good wish and every tender thought,

Believe me, Always yours,
H.B.T.

t know why it was not until then that there was any mention of
's knighthood, as the Honours List must have come out long
ly. I know I did genuinely resent it, believing with Max that
oods had now become so common as to be more a penalty than a
on. I would have had no objection to a baronetcy.
ncident of the sweetpeas must have set Oliver thinking, for it was
er that that he asked me point blank whether he had my whole
. Since, however perverted my conduct, I am a fairly truthful
confessed that he did not, and as he was not inclined for a half loaf,
engagement came to an end, much, I am sure, to his family's relief.
think that I should ever have been very bien vue as the châtelaine of
Castle, which would eventually have been his.
ver upset this may have caused me was soon forgotten in the
us joy of having Herbert to stay at Landford whilst he was on tour
g at Southampton. I accompanied him in to every performance,
ves to and fro – some twelve miles – were all too short. My mother,
nt from his letters, always gave him a very kind welcome. Indeed
real liking for him, as he for her. There was only one year's
in their ages, though she used always to refer to him as 'the Old
' – at fifty-seven this seems rather an inaccurate description, and
tful in its emphasis on the difference in our ages.

Olivia at 21. John Galsworthy and many other celebrities were at the party Tree gave for her.

1910 and 1911

It was now arranged that I should go out and spend the winter months with my brother in India. He disapproved of the humdrum life at Landford for a young girl, and generously offered for me to come as his guest, of course accompanied by Wiltshire. There were tremendous preparations in the way of clothes – a regular trousseau of startling dresses – huge hats in even larger boxes, and tin lined cases to contain the trunks, and of course a topee, then *de rigueur*. What a contrast to a similar journey today!

I sailed from Tilbury in a P & O ship, and as I mounted the gangway I found myself being eyed by a good-looking soldierly man in his forties. What he saw he evidently approved, and within a very few days he had asked me to marry him. Neither then nor later did he appeal to me – also I liked the figure of the ship's doctor who started buzzing round, and also proposed to me. I did not go so far as to accept him, but I spent some very flirtatious hours in his surgery, whither I repaired for treatment for a sore throat. Under the influence of Galsworthy I toyed with the notion of marrying him and assisting him in tending the poor of an East End practice. This altruistic idea was interrupted by his going on shore at Port Said and getting distinctly drunk. My other admirer was leaving the ship there, and on my return I found him patiently waiting with some gifts he had bought me. He had not improved his pursuit by coming into my cabin when we were passing Stromboli, to take me up to see its eruption, and, not knowing that Wiltshire was sharing my cabin, by mistake endeavouring to embrace her ardently!

Having seen him depart from the ship at Port Said, incredible as it may seem, I then and there went to remonstrate with the doctor for his insobriety. To pursue a man to his cabin at midnight and expect no emotional reaction would be crazy enough, but to go after one already 'bottled' was indeed asking for trouble, which I duly got, and was only rescued from the 'fate worse than death' by the arrival of the faithful Wiltshire. Quite unable to recognise that the result was mostly my fault I was furious with him, and refused to speak to him till we were nearing Bombay. Being very bored I found it difficult to keep up. As is so often the way with shipboard affairs, when I saw him on land I realised what an impossible and ridiculous business the whole thing had been, but it was very rough on him, as it was some while before he grasped that there was no future for him.

After driving through the picturesque bazaars of Bombay we commenced the long journey up country, and at length arrived at our destination at Lahore where my brother had rented a bungalow for Christmas 'week'. I have very little recollection of our days there, a whirl of polo and dances among a crowd of people all strange to me and intimate with each other. I know that at the end my brother quite suddenly announced our departure for Sialkot where his regiment – the 12th Lancers – was stationed, and gave us hardly any time to get my trousseau back into its trunks. When we arrived at the bungalow which Billy had taken specially for my advent, it was quite unprepared for our unexpected descent. Tired out and disappointed, we could only roll ourselves in a blanket and go to sleep. Next morning Billy had to be off to his regimental duties without being able to give us either help or instruction. At home I had had no experience whatever of housekeeping, beyond handing out stores to the cook, and was entirely at sea in this oriental set-up. Nobody came to my rescue, and I felt rather lost and miserable. In course of time I got used to it, and the little white bed in the middle of the shiny floor, and the bathroom with its tin bath filled with the water brought in by the sweeper in kerosene tins.

In due course I was initiated into station life. The military world always remained alien to me – I had no contact point with subalterns, though I tried my hardest to learn something about the horses and polo prospects which formed their conversation. However it was not very long before two of them attached themselves to me. One was a senior major, who for years had been enamoured of a certain lady who had travelled on the same ship with me, and with whom I had made friends. She had not come straight north, but was staying with people elsewhere. Pending her arrival Cecil put in some very good work with me. He was decidedly what is known as a 'ladies' man', well read, including French literature, a pleasant companion who studied one's moods, and introduced gallant speeches (often in French). We used to ride together before breakfast.

My other follower was a very rugged Tasmanian, ugly, very vital, very cheery, a magnificent polo player. It is difficult to know what attraction he can have had for me except his devotion, his honesty, and a boyish exuberance. He was also a very good dancer, and matched me well. There is a photograph of me leaning on the rails at a local race meeting with one of these stalwarts on either side of me.

After a while Cecil's lady friend turned up, and he had the difficult task of conducting a double pursuit. For a time he showed considerable skill at this, and I continued to enjoy very soulful love-making in semi-French on the verandah, till one day he slipped up and put two identical declarations of devotion into one envelope – I think it was mine. His lady friend and I got together, countersigned them, and returned them to him! I was so annoyed that I thereupon consented to marry the Tasmanian, 'Nikola'.

My time in India was drawing to an end, but before we left my brother made up a foursome of a lady he was pursuing with dishonourable intentions, Nikola and me, and motored up to Peshawar. We chose a selection of things from the bazaar to be sent to the hotel, and then proceeded to explore the Khyber Pass. When we returned to Peshawar we found that a Hindu-Moslem row had broken out in our absence and when we got to the hotel we learned that the goods we had chosen at the bazaar merchants' had all been looted.

The moment had come for our farewells – an impassioned scene under the sweet-scented orange flowers surrounding our bungalow, with 'Nikola', who was to go to Tasmania where his father had a sheep farm, to get his consent, and financial support, for our marriage.

I left India without regrets – I have no call of the East in me – the poverty of the half-starved crowds of natives, the dirt, the flies, the cruel ill-usage of the animals – all revolted me. Like most tourists at the time of the British Raj, I met hardly any Indians and learned nothing about them and their problems. The little clusters of silly men and women occupied with their sports and their love affairs only aimed at importing English chintzes and keeping themselves as uncontaminated as possible by the age-old aristocrats among whom they dwelt. I am not of course referring to the District Officers, who did wonderful work, whom I never met either.

My voyage home was unmarred by complications with any male whatever, though I met a woman who became a life-long friend. Somewhere near Port Said we passed the P & O liner going in the opposite direction and which had my doctor friend on board – I was thankful he was not still on our ship. During the summer he turned up to see me at Landford, when I behaved with disgraceful cowardice, having no doubt a very bad conscience, and left my mother to entertain him. I have no doubt that the first thing I did on my return, Nikola or no Nikola, was to throw myself into Herbert's arms!

Things at home went on much the same, which meant more debts, but we boasted a chef in the kitchen, and a kennel-maid to look after the thirteen poodles, who had their own rice pudding daily.

Cyril now owned a garage in Romsey which he was making pay fairly well, but had come to the conclusion that I was out of reach, and sought consolation by marrying a little music-hall artiste on whom he vented his spleen about me.

'Nikola' had duly gone off to Tasmania to see his father, and a very prolonged silence ensued. I could not understand this as he had been writing to me daily. Eventually news arrived that his father, so far from augmenting his allowance to enable him to marry, would stop it altogether if he did – he would consent only if Nikola left the army and went to live out there. I did not feel myself cut out for sheep farming, and so once more the idea of my marrying was abandoned. From the reference in the letters from Herbert which follow it is evident that I kept him quite *au fait* with what was going on. He, no more than I, seemed to see no reason why my connection with him should make any bar to matrimony! Looking back now, I cannot think why, as long as he lived I did not stick to him alone, but I am afraid my experimental nature, which always causes me to try everything once, urged me to sample wife- and motherhood, nor could I resist the temptation to have a *cavaliere servente* buzzing round. I do not excuse this weakness, a very bad one, I only admit it.

Two letters from Herbert follow – the second referring to the exit of 'Nikola'.

July 19   Marienbad

My dear Olivia,

Thank you for your delightful letter – but it always joys me to hear from you. I am so glad to hear all your news of yourself, your garden, your mother and your dogs. For myself, I have no adventures – I have been occupied most of my time in working – I am doing a sort of essay on Henry VIII and his time, which will, I think, be interesting. I have wonderful news from London – I have just had a windfall of £5000! And there is something in the wind (which has not yet fallen) more important still. I think Henry will be fine. I had already thought of the choir in the Situation of Wolsey's fall – you will see! I mean to let the gorgeous robe fall in the Court – then to go up to the Chapel door and knock – it is opened by a monk – I pass through and the choir is heard. So you see 'les beaux esprits', etc.

It is awful to-day – most depressing, not to say suicidal – I shall plunge into a mud-bath by way of a diversion! . . .

God bless you!

Ever your friend,
Herbert B.T.

September 23   His Majesty's Theatre

My dear,

  I am greatly distressed to hear your news – you are indeed unlucky in these affairs – how I wish I could bring your fairy prince into being! But perhaps, as your mother says, it is not an unmixed evil.

  I am so sorry it will be impossible for me to come to you on Sunday, as I had long promised myself to Maxine Elliott who has to leave England next week and has made special arrangements for me. I have heard from Claude [Tree's eldest son by May Reed] who I hope will be happy in his temporary home – his address is 28 Rue Reservoirs, Compiègne.

  When do you come again to London? I will try to get to you on a week day, if I can.

  The children return to London next week – Viola, as you know, is in Milan.

  What are you going to write to the young man? Do tell me.

  Dear, I am terribly sorry – don't fret. I am just called – so I close.

Your devoted,

H

By November Olivia seems to have recovered, and together with her friend the prankster 'Cockie' Alexander, she had a mad scheme to dress up as an old lady and try and take Herbert in. This was how she described the affair to Miss Mackay.

November 27   Landford Manor, Salisbury

. . . At 12 I retired to Clarksons and was made-up as an old widow – and then proceeded to His Majesty's (where I had arranged with Herbert to see 'my friend') and sent up a bogus card – He came down to see me in the royal room which was nearly dark, and then led me thro' into the auditorium which was quite so. He said 'you know Miss Truman?' I said I did 'Eccentric isn't she?' I said 'Do you think so? – she is very fond of you isn't she' 'Well' he said 'I think she is rather designing – rather what I call a minx!!' – I gasped! – Then I said 'My nephew used to act with you – Robert Taber – how sad his death was!' 'Yes' said Herbert 'You know that he was supposed to be Miss Truman's lover' – I gasped again. 'No' I cried 'I did not think she was like that!' I then begged him to kiss me once – it being my one long cherished ambition 'I don't think I can' he demurred – 'You see I promised Miss Truman to be faithful to her – and she is so passionate' – I begged him not to refuse me 'Then too' he continued 'I belong to a sort of Masonic society called the Hermits and all that sort of thing is forbidden' 'But if you can kiss her you can kiss me!' I cried and burst into tears – whereupon my beloved laughed and told me he had known all along from the second he saw me, which shows how *very* early in the morning one would have to get up to deceive him!! – I *was* disappointed – but it makes me *scream* to think of us sitting side by side in the stalls talking nonsense!! He then went and fetched Cockie who was waiting in the vestibule, and was too nice and charming – It is always a joy to see him – no one can compare with him . . .

Then in the midst of a season's hunting, Olivia wrote:

December 10   The Querns, Cirencester

. . . It was on Wednesday I left London, and not till last Sunday did I see Herbert in private – and then only for 10 minutes. He swore solemnly that there was nothing behind his altered behaviour – so I suppose it is just that he has no further use for me – poor me, what wasted devotion! – But he told me that his wife had opened one of my letters to him!! – a pretty kettle of fish, with a tongue like hers!! still she can only say what everyone else says already so I try not to worry. The latest on dit is that she drinks. Walter Creighton [a member of Tree's company with whom Olivia was friendly] was talking to me about Herbert, and said he believed him to be quite devoid of all friendship or affection, save the paternal instinct which he had ad nauseum!! – the prodigal father!! – but then Walter has hardly a large enough scope of mind to understand that of my lord . . .

She saw Herbert once more in 1910, and afterwards left with her brother Ivor for a short winter-sports holiday in Switzerland.

Xmas Eve   Hotel Chamossaire, Chesières

. . . I left home on Saturday and saw 'Henry' that afternoon – Also my dear lord who was very well and happy and gracious with congratulations pouring in. He seemed to like the silver cornered blotting pad I gave him – his 'tear blotter' he called it . . . Then I went to hear the music at the Oratory, excellent as usual, and after tea for a drive with Herbert who was again in a charming mood . . .

And he wrote to her for Christmas:

December 24   His Majesty's Theatre

I wired you telling you how sorry I was to be so out of sorts.

I hope you will have a lovely Christmas. I am sending you a little remembrance, but it will take some days before it arrives.

I was to have gone to Paris, where at the Opera they are putting on Macbeth specially for me and Bourchier. He has gone over, however. [Arthur Bourchier, a fellow actor manager, often appeared with Tree, though they were seldom on good terms.] My wife and Felicity are joining Viola in Milan . . . I shall be a bachelor. Claude is here and perhaps we shall all three meet soon. Let me know when you come to town and will arrange a little feast – there will probably be one on the 11th January (the 150th performance).

. . . Thank you for all your sweetness and unchanging kindness to me. Give my affectionate wishes to your mother – and believe me always,

Your devoted,
Herbert

For some years I had been in the habit of staying with a distant relative in Gloucester Place, Portman Square. With her I met a fairly well known singer, Alys Bateman, who developed a deep affection for me, and interested herself in teaching me singing – whether the idea that I had a voice was hers or mine I do not know – in either case I think it was probably erroneous, and anyhow, how could anyone who had no gift for the piano and so could not play her accompaniments at practice, and who was already rather deaf, hope to succeed? But like every other fad of mine, this had to be given way to, and to her flat in Victoria Street I used to repair for lessons. To this also went a Canadian baritone, Edmund Burke – a man of fine proportions and coarse good looks, who quickly added himself to my collection. I remember thinking it very romantic when he knelt and kissed my foot, being much too stupid to realise that he was no doubt repeating some of his operatic 'business'. Again, I preened myself when at an evening reception at which he was singing he chose 'Bid me to live, and I will live thy protestant to be' and directed it to me.

I now took it into my head to go to Paris for the training of my probably mythical voice. A family was found willing to receive me, and I set out accompanied by Wiltshire. My hostesses' apartment was situated in the Avenue Kléber, one of the roads radiating from the Etoile. The family consisted of a mother and three daughters. The mother composed music – an opera of hers was actually performed whilst I was there. The eldest daughter was a religious fanatic and always in church, the second gave lessons, and the youngest, a plump pleasant young woman, was supposed to 'companion' me.

The reason for my presence in Paris being to sing, I duly began work with two teachers – why two? – a most attractive lady who sang at the Opéra Comique, and a retired basso from the Grand Opera. Neither of these experts succeeded in making a job of me – I might have got on better if my male mentor had been a handsome tenor! Actually whilst I was at the Avenue Kléber, my baritone adorer turned up again. I think the Opéra Comique lady was his friend and introduction. I went about with him a little, and he took me to Maxim's – a tremendously daring adventure for an unmarried girl.

An extract from a letter to Miss Mackay at this time – it was now the spring of 1911 – shows that much of Edmund Burke's attraction for Olivia was a supposed likeness to Herbert.

March 29   In the train

. . . Certainly for the moment I am most idiotically in love with him, and he grows more and more absurdly like my beloved lord! . . .

As has been seen, Herbert's eldest boy, Claude, had been sent to a tutor at St Cloud – I have no idea why – and I thought it would be kind to ask him up to Paris for the day. He was a difficult, moody boy, who bitterly resented his illegitimacy and was the only one of Herbert's children who never did any good for himself. I associated males with horses, and thought he might enjoy the Concours Hippique, and accordingly took seats for it. Claude turned out hardly to know which end of a horse went first, and cared less. The fine points of the jumping competition bored him to hysteria, just as his companionship bored me! The only reward I got for my pains was an angry reprimand from Herbert for disturbing the boy's studies.

Shortly after this Herbert himself came over with Claude's mother a little while before she had their last child. I was asked to dine with them and go to some play Herbert wanted to see. I had not met May before, and was much struck by her handsome looks, and the dignity which she showed in her difficult position. For over twenty years she devoted herself entirely to him and their children with a fidelity that many of the married women who cold-shouldered her lacked. We made an odd trio that night – people unaware of our identity would doubtless have supposed Herbert and May to be husband and wife, and me her daughter. From then onwards I used to see her regularly. I think it does us both credit that we exhibited no jealousy, particularly she of me, for she must have been well aware that I gave Herbert much that she could not. Not only was she not an intellectual woman, but she had not much interest in the theatre, and sometimes I believe did not see him in his plays. This was utterly incomprehensible to me, knowing how much he and his art were one, and that not to understand and sympathise with one was not to understand or sympathise with the other. The fact I am afraid remains that, fond as he was of her, and much as he respected her integrity of character, she often bored him!

There follows Olivia's account of all this at the time:

April 8   63 Avenue Kléber, Paris

. . . Claude – Herbert's boy – has been up here most of the week. He is a dreadful person to take about tho', as nothing in the world interests him, nor pictures, nor books, nor plays, nor horses (I took him to the Concours Hippique to see some good hacks and some jumping, one afternoon), nor even food!! – I think he is a little wanting, and that he will come to a bad end, especially as he can sign Herberts name so that he can't himself tell it from his own signature! – He has no love either for my dear lord who has been kindness itself to him . . .

April 25   63 Avenue Kléber, Paris

. . . I have been thro' a terrible week since I last wrote owing to the accidental discovery that Edmund instead of leaving Paris on the Wednesday as he said he was obliged to do, stayed on two more days without telling me . . . I demanded an explanation . . . he declared that he did not see me because he was losing his head which must at any cost be avoided until his home affairs are settled up. (They are bad at present – the whole responsibility of his mother, father and sister rests on his shoulders, and the former has to undergo a serious operation). But he finished by saying that altho' for the present things must perforce remain as they are between us he loved me with an 'affectionate and lasting love' . . . Alack! a day, that ever I should live entirely for a man again, as I live in and for him – None of them are worth it, and it makes one suffer so. He has mounted the Olympian pinnacle where Herbert reigned alone – Herbert – he arrived in Paris last week!! – he came to see me unexpectidly one evening, found me engulfed in tears, but only stayed 5 minutes!! – He had Putney with him and also Claude! – Then what must he do but get laid up by gout, so I saw very little of him, but Saturday evening he asked me to join 'them' at the play, and one of these girls and I went! – So his woman and I have met at last! – She certainly is very good looking, very nice too, with a particularly pleasing voice, but if you will credit it she is on the point of foaling again! – God knows how many that makes, and going about with a grown up son I call it indecent. As for Herbert I call it both scandalous and disgusting of him and most unfair to his lawful children. There are limits to everything, and he is far too old for this. It degrades his whole character. But I suppose it is no affair of mine. He left on Sunday to join Viola at Turin. I saw him for a few minutes that morning. He leaves Putney and a doctor he brought over for her, behind. I met her in the street yesterday! What Mother and Edmund would say about it all I dread to think!!

Back in England, and with Burke still in tow, Olivia was preparing to take part in the Shakespeare Ball, a big costume occasion at the Albert Hall, in which Lady Tree took a leading part.

Tuesday, May 30   In the train

. . . I therefore went about the business of collecting my kit for the Shakespeare ball. I also looked in at His Majesty's and saw Herbert for two minutes in the middle of the stage in the middle of rehearsal which confused me very much as Walter Creighton and Margery Maude ect: were all there, and must have thought it odd . . .

June 13   Landford Manor, Salisbury

. . . Last week was full of agitations connected with my dancing in the Tree quadrille, as I could by no means get any answers at all out of Edmund and then nothing but grumbles about his work and his health, and his doubts about taking part in it after all. On Friday I rushed up to a rehearsal at the Duke of Rutlands – which was a very humourous performance – tho' I was too anxious trying to pick up the very confusing steps to see it at the time, especially as D'Egville picked me, the only serious member of the company – to make all his satirical remarks to! Dancing masters always do!! – of course Edmund did not turn up – nor did I see him at all – and then he wrote and said he didn't wish to be in it – so I sent in our resignation to Lady Tree – and suffered tortures thro' the certainty that he does not love me or he could not treat me so casually – Having reconciled myself to being out of it – I hear from him this morning that he went to a rehearsal yesterday on his own, and is apparently going to take private lessons! This shilly-shallying is very maddening, but I suppose unless one is on the spot it is hard to realise all his work and preoccupations . . . When he gets more used to his present life he will also no doubt settle down into Herberts calmer state of mind . . .

Then this description of the gala at His Majesty's to celebrate the coronation of King George V and Queen Mary.

July 2   Landford Manor, Salisbury

Dearest Aunt Judy,

I was so glad to get your most sympathetic letter – I daresay you are right in what you say but it is difficult to take a hopeful and general view of life from the inside of its mincing machine! – all this disappointment and unhappiness may in the end have a very benefical effect – but I fear the contrary result –

My last letter was I think posted on my arrival in London on Monday, when I went straight to the dress-rehearsal of the gala at His Majesty's – I had then very little hope of getting to the actual performance – it lasted until after four o'clock – and then I went to tea with Edmund who was very nice and fascinating . . . In the evening we saw the 'Only Way' at which I hoped to weep, but remained quite unmoved! Next day I took Mrs Burke [Edmund's mother] and Suzette Potter [the daughter of Herbert's box-office manager] to the White City, where they have a very interesting exhibition this year of native workers of all countries and also most artistically set scenes of various cities – I was taken back to India and many happy memories. That night was the gala for which Herbert was dear enough to send me a much coveted 10 guinea seat – but I think it was only right that I, who love his welfare more than all the rest put together – should be with him at so important a moment. It was a beautiful scene. The theatre was decorated with garlands of green leaves with gold fruit and bindings, caught up by large gold bows – the procenium was surrounded and garlanded with crimson roses – with a centre piece of the royal arms in stained glass illuminated from behind as the King entered – and from high gold columns at each side fell another shower of red blossoms – I could not see the King from where I sat in the upper circle but the general effect of the uniforms and diamonds even in the gallery, was very striking –

On the stage every walking part was taken by an actor of note, but I agree with the 'Pall Mall' that excepts from plays the context of which is unfamiliar to foreigners was not a happy choice, and that Granville Barker overdid the noisiness of the 'Julius Caesar' crowd – why Herbert who created stage crowds should leave that for a junior to manage I can't conceive – The only really perfect thing was my dear lords own work the 'Vision of Delight' – that struck the right note, and was indeed the most exquisite thing you can conceive. When at the end the 1,000 persons on the stage, and the whole house joined in the national anthem it was a very stirring moment. The prologue was grand too given by Forbes-Robertson whose voice thrilled one by its beauty – the line 'so stand you crowned to serve yr country's need, no King of shadows, but a King indeed' – I thought splendid. It was the first time I had seen 'David Garrick' Wyndham and Mary Moore I thought still astonishingly young, but the piece rather dull horse-play. It was an unforgettable evening . . .

In August 1911 Olivia and her mother went to Bad Ems in Germany to try another cure for Olivia's incipient deafness.

August 25   Hotel d'Angleterre, Bad Ems

. . . Herbert arrived almost at the same moment as me, having escaped from rehearsal for a few minutes only and he took me with him to look at a picture of the Macbeth witches by Fuseli which had been given him, and was at Weedon Grossmiths house in Bedford Square which is nice and full of lovely things. We passed by Edmunds late lodgings which was a curious and rather painful coincidence. In the afternoon I shopped, went and sang to Parlovitz (who was very pleased with my voice) – and then went to His Majesty's where of course Herbert kept me waiting ages. However I found, Comyns Carr, Raymond Blathwayt, Walter Creighton, and a pleasant woman called Mrs Delvaux, there so I was quite amused. Afterwards I drove him half way out to Putney (!!) – he looks very well indeed, and was most kind. 'Macbeth' I am glad to say promises excellently . . .

September 8   Hotel d'Angleterre, Bad Ems

. . . Of course the greatest event of the last 10 days is the prodigious success of my dear lord in 'Macbeth' – Tho' his triumphs always thrill me, this one does so especially, as I was rather dubious about it, the heroic not being his strong point. He must be quite wonderful, as I don't think I have ever seen so unanimously enthusiastic a press – I count the moments till I

can see it, and loathe everyone else who is able to do so! – The evening of
the first night I sat alone in the garden by the river, so as to be with him in
spirit as much as possible. Mr Potter wired me news of its tremendous
reception, and then next morning when I went down to the Brunnen his
name in great letters on the posters greeted my eyes – I can't think how I
avoided committing an absurdity I was so foolishly exultantly happy! – I
could have hugged anyone I saw – There wasn't a cloud in the sky and all
the world sang . . .

There seems to have been only one letter from Tree in 1911. It is dated March 14th.

My dear,
        How are you? Better I hope by now.
    Thanks for your sweet letter. There is a terrible rush here but I must send
you this line to let you know I am not forgetting you in the din.

                                            Ever yours,
                                                H

Write!

1912

A long gap except for a number of the hundred and fifty telegrams I had from him occurs, and generally means that I was seeing him in London, till the January of the following year, 1912, when I received this from His Majesty's Theatre:

My dear,

I have been hard at work *all* day long, without a moment's pause, and now after the play, I have been working incessantly. I am sorry I could not come. Can you manage to come to rehearsal in the morning? I begin at 11. Do try. I hope you are reposing pleasantly.

Ever yours,
H

Olivia, again engaged on a season's hunting, was profoundly shocked at Tree's appearance on the music halls.

January 23   Kings Head Hotel, Cirencester

. . . In the evening I went to 'Orpheus' which is improved out of all knowledge. It is now full of life and 'go', and Viola in place of the elephantine American [the mistress of an American newspaperman in Paris], is a very joy to behold, so lovely, and charming – her singing too is delicious – The house was very full – We had the royal box (I took Minnie and Wiltshire) and Herbert joined us at intervals, but seemed too preoccupied for conversation. I had a long talk with Viola, who was more than nice to me, and full of indignation that her father would not allow her to be 'puffed' as she deserves – it certainly seems unjust that simply because she is in their own theatre, she should be deprived of the advantages she would reap elsewhere. Nowadays peoples careers are only made by going on telling the public that they are 'it' as the Americans say. And I'm sure he is no longer in a posistion to give himself airs. Of course she is furious over this music-hall affair which she calls so futile even financially since it is not assured income but only like a sum won gambling, which he will have spent or lost in six months. How dreadful to barter so much honor for so much dross! – I feel worse and worse about it, and can really think of nothing else. To see his name staring at one in giant letters on omnibuses when all these years he has avoided these vulgarities alone of all the actors, makes me wince every time. And everyone condemns him, if some excuse him – and to hear him thus adversely criticised on all sides is torture to me. He who so proudly wrote '– – stoop to expediency and honor dies' and 'many there are – – who pandering to the towns decadent taste barter the precious pearl for gawdy paste' – should so descend. Could I have known before it was too late, how I would have thrown myself at his feet, and begged him not to do it – if only I had had the money behind me to double his salary and buy him off. I have said nothing to him – since this horrible thing is done, never to be undone – it is useless so to vex him – but what I have done is to write and warn him to beware of the flattering toadies blind to his ideals and his highest interests – with whom I feel he is surrounded, and who have urged him on to this crime against himself. He is become very intolerant of contradiction or of any difference of opinion – he is contemptuous of those who do not agree with him – And because I love him so deeply and am so jealous for his reputation I feel all this and suffer – What he will say to so daring an attack I do not know or care. I have always spoken what was in my mind to him, and I love him too well to do otherwise now whatever it costs me or however vain it may be . . .

I must to bed – in 'thy oraisons be all my sins remembered' – but don't let me keep you up all night!

OMT

To think that even now Herbert is doing his 'turn' between acrobats and comic singers!

February 4   King's Head Hotel, Cirencester

. . . Have you seen the cartoon of Herbert in 'Punch'? – I think it is just what he deserves – but it makes me writhe to look at – that he should have exposed himself to such a thing! should make himself a but of laughter for the whole country – I wish I could get over it – but I can't at all . . .

February 12   In the train

Dearest Aunt Judy,

     I was so glad to hear that you were able to go to 'Orpheus' on Wednesday, and that you enjoyed it so much. I was sure Viola would fascinate you in it – Herbert is certainly full of mental versatility – I am very interested in his 'Othello' production, tho' I do not fancy him as the Moor – perhaps being at the 'halls' has given him a taste for blackening his face, and he may wish to qualify by gradual stages for bones on the Brighton beach! The Neilson Terry girl, tho' somewhat lacking in temperament, should prove a good engagement, being of the massive build which looks well on that big stage. Lawrence Irving should certainly be excellent if he is like his brother, who you and I saw together as Iago – the only part I have ever really liked him in . . .

My mother had now turned completely against Landford, lovely as it was. I do not know why, except that as usual we were living beyond our means. She thought it a good idea to take a house near Cirencester from which my brother and I could hunt, but it was not a modest hunting box she chose, but rather an enormous mansion called Eastcourt House, halfway between Malmesbury and Cirencester, about as remote a spot as could be found anywhere, which nearly drove her distracted with boredom when we came to live there.

We had not been long at Eastcourt when my Major from the outward voyage to India turned up, still hoping he might persuade me to think better of my refusal to marry him. Mother rather approved of him and his looks and his good breeding, but he made not the slightest appeal to me. He had already taken me out whilst I was staying with my cousin in London, and on bringing me home after a theatre had attacked me with such violence as to loosen my hair – mercifully, just as my faithful maid had rescued me from the ship's doctor, so my cousin's faithful butler, a great character, rescued me from the Major. Still nothing daunted, whilst at Eastcourt he invaded my room in the night, which made me perfectly furious, not only on grounds of propriety but because my face was covered with grease. This led to his final dismissal and shortly afterwards he found someone else to marry.

The next *prétendant* was an elderly man of cadaverous appearance who had for years been in love with a very charming friend of mine – incidentally the mother of David Niven the film star. Tommy's subsequently published letters to his Egeria are really beautiful. Just as Herbert kept urging me to 'commit matrimony', Etta urged Tommy to do the same thing. I do not know how an alliance between two people both having a romantic interest in someone else would have worked, but anyhow she persuaded him that it was worth trying.

He was both clever and amusing, and I enjoyed the opening gambits of his courtship. Subsequently, when war came, Etta's husband was posted among those missing, and with the removal of this obstacle, she recalled her swain and married him.

Meanwhile the 'background music' went on as before. Herbert came to stay at Eastcourt, and as usual filled me with happiness. His visit coincided with that of Cyril Maude's daughter, Margery, a schoolfellow of mine who also had rather a penchant for him. [Cyril Maude was a well-known actor.]

During the summer of 1912 Viola Tree was married to Alan Parsons, a young man only recently down from Oxford. She had had several very splendid offers and her parents were a little disappointed in her decision. Herbert never became really attached to Alan. He refers to the wedding in the following letters:

June 30   His Majesty's Theatre

My very dear Olivia,

Thank you for your sweet letter. I must try to reach you before I leave which will be about the 15th July. Are you coming to Viola's wedding, and have you received an invitation? If not, I will send one.

This has been an awful year for me, but I am hopeful of the Autumn. 'Drake' is, I think, likely to be a popular success, and I can do other things during its progress.

I hope you will be very, very happy in your new home – it sounds attractive.

Viola and Iris have just returned – both looking radiantly well. Viola is very happy among her presents . . .

You *must marry soon.*

Bless you, dear.

Yours ever,
Herbert

The wedding was a big and amusing one, and Herbert in great spirits. He even went so far as to make mock love to Marie Corelli, whose looks were not her strong point, and she took him seriously enough to resent it, upon which Herbert remarked 'Thus does one tear one's trousers on the barbed wire of love!' The poor lady seems rather to have inspired wit, as Lady Tree also made up an amusing verse about her, which went:

A little too young for her age
A little too stockingly blue

A little too wise to be sage
A little too good to be true.

Herbert's pleasure in the goodwill shown to them on the occasion of the marriage is testified to by this letter, addressed to Eastcourt House. He refers to my 'committing a play' – the first of a long series of indiscretions, it was a mere election-time sketch. Whilst still at Landford, I had written one in which my future husband appeared as a powdered footman looking very handsome indeed.

August 13   Brussels

Thank you for your charming letter. I am now on my way home and shall hope to see you very soon – either in London or better still at your new home – you are sure to have made it beautiful by now.

I have had a wonderful time for health and reflection. I have managed to write something which I think you will like – in the philosophic strain.

Yes, Viola's wedding was indeed a wonderful event and I was very proud to think that all those dear people took the trouble to come out to see us. It is beautiful to think that we have won their affections by being ourselves all these years. Yes, I hope my dear Viola will be very happy – she has a wonderful disposition – quite apart from any other mortal I know. To me she has always been sweet and kind and she has a firmness of character and an aloof yet joyous outlook on things which are indeed enviable.

Fancy you having committed a play! That is indeed courageously enterprising – you must let me see it or read it to me.

Drake I think is going to be a winner. I think the play admirable and just the right thing for the moment in England. But I could not play the part with the necessary ebullient and breezy sincerity – so I am sure I have done the right thing for the public and my artistic conscience in withdrawing myself from its pleasant glare.

I have had a pretty strenuous time and now I must make money for the sake of everybody. I must *smear* myself with gold – that is the feeling I have!

God bless you my sweet friend.

Ever yours,
Herbert B. Tree

It is a very charming tribute to his daughter. The affection between them was very deep, which of course always drew me to her. There is only one more letter that year, though he paid us the visit promised in it, and I was as blissfully happy as ever in his company.

September 5   His Majesty's Theatre

My dear Olivia,

    Thank you for your most kind wish that I should come and I have made up my mind to do so, although I am terribly worried here – not (thank Heaven!) about Theatre matters which are going splendidly. Indeed Drake promises to rival Henry VIII and without me too, which is an enormous achievement as it will show that His Majesty's can be run without me!

    I am delighted that you were pleased. Yes, Lynn Harding is a most excellent acquisition for the part – my only regret is that he cannot long stay in the cast. You are wrong about the extravagant salary. I was sorry to part with him before – but I considered the action wise – it is of course very difficult for those outside the theatre to judge of its internal policy. I have just refused £4000 to open at the Alhambra. As to the other (the Northern tour of variety theatres) I think it was quite wise – I needed the money and I could not (alas!) afford to be ruined.

    I will wire you when I shall arrive. I am terribly sorry about the muddle on Tuesday. I could not arrange as Lady Tree was ill – and I had a few men friends at the Carlton including Lloyd George.

    Pray accept my very contrite apologies. I should have enjoyed the little supper above all things. Please tell your friend [almost certainly Etta Niven] who is most delightful how sorry I was, and forgive me.

                                    Yours affectionately,
                                    Herbert

In October Olivia went to Drake and took as her escort a friend from Landford days, a sporting character who had done a good deal in teaching her to ride.

    . . . I found that my beloved one, had not after all gone to Genoa, as poor Viola has lost her voice, and had to delay her debut – he came in and saw me – being himself voiceless, and looking ill and tired in a morning suit – On seeing the Farmer he dragged me into the royal room, and asked if I were alone in London with that 'fellow from the country' – I said I was alone at my club – why not? – He then asked what I intended doing – I said 'going to bed of course' – he then accused me of contemplating sleeping with Farmer and would not believe the contrary until I swore it on oath and protested that he should not judge everyone by himself!!!

    As a matter of fact, my night was a disturbed one, as the chill in my tummy got bad and gave me a hell of a time – I was also worried about

Herbert, as I always am when he is unwell – I can bear him being seperated from me when his health and spirits are good, but to leave him alone in the dome when he is seedy, maddens me – I longed to tuck him up in bed with hot drinks, and generally fuss over him – I relieved my feelings in a long and passionate letter! . . .

In December Tree was off to America:

December 6   Eastcourt, Malmesbury

. . . I saw my beloved Lord twice before he sailed for America last Saturday – which I thought was sweet of him in the middle of all his preparations – Once he ran into Gloucester Place, and Friday morning I visited him in the dome where his dresser was struggling with piles of suits and boxes, and his secretary trying vainly to get him to attend to a whole table full of papers! – I sent him a most passionate wire to the boat, which so touched him that he answered it – It is glorious to think that I was one of the very last people of whom he thought. I fear the poor darling has had a shocking passage, and he *is* such a vile sailor. He returns on the 17th (his birthday) – He wants to see whether it would be wise for him to take a company over there . . .

1913

I think it was in the early days of 1913 that I was again hunting from Cirencester, and was spending a few nights with some friends there when I met a man who was to affect my life far more than any of the previous ones who had been mixed with it. My feelings for them, as has been seen, were never very deep; Harry I really cared for, though not of course to the exclusion of Herbert. When I met him he was commanding the 2nd Battalion of the Gordon Highlanders, but was actually an Irishman of the most Irish, with all their traditional charm, wit and imagination. He was married to a woman considerably his senior, one of the kindest and most motherly people imaginable, whom everyone liked, but who was quite unable to keep up with the ardent and mercurial temperament of her husband. She therefore had the extreme wisdom to leave him complete liberty to follow his fancy in the many directions it took him; the result was that their deep fundamental affection remained unimpaired, and that no matter in whose pursuit he was engaged, her wishes and convenience always came first. In fact I have never seen a more considerate husband.

He arrived in Cirencester for a few days' hunting, and escorted me when I went out either hacking or to hounds, I forget which, but I know that when we returned, and I had bathed and had got into a rather seductive specimen of what was then known as a 'tea gown', we foregathered in front of the fire, and as I lay on the sofa he lost no time in telling me that he had fallen under my spell, and I knew that within limits I responded. That was the beginning of our friendship, though I did not have the opportunity of seeing him very often as, his leave up, he had to return to his regiment which was stationed in Cairo. When he said goodbye it had been arranged that I should go and stay with the Uniackes for two or three months the following winter, a most unwise arrangement.

Meanwhile, as we can see from the letters that follow, Olivia was occupied with such events as a shopping expedition with Tree, and is seeing a good deal of her friend Etta

115

Niven and the politician Tommy Platt who was dividing his attentions between Etta and Olivia.

January 11   Eastcourt, Malmesbury

. . . I *did* go up on Tuesday, and had a very busy days sale shopping. I lunched with my beloved lord at the Automobile Club – he was charming to me – and afterwards took me into Bond Street, and gave me Xmas presents! Both of them give me great joy – one is a golden orange with scent inside it to hang on one's bracelet – which was copied from Wolsey's in 'Henry VIII' and so specially suitable for him to give me – the other is Asprey's new little charm – the bluebird of happiness in a little gold cage – I hope it may have some effect on my fortunes! – any how as I told him, so long as it symbolises his loving wishes for me – I can never be entirely unhappy.

January 24   Eastcourt, Malmesbury

. . . Etta came and picked me up at Gloucester Place, and we dined together, going on to the Coliseum where Tommy joined us later having just knocked a man over in his taxi! . . . After the show we went on to the Capitol Hotel, where Herbert had a supper in a private room – prior to his departure to Russia for a fortnight – He summoned me *five* times on the phone, *and* by wire, so conclude he wanted to see me! – Were present a son of old Evelyn Wood's, who was in the Remount dept. and has now gone on the music hall stage, and his wife, a very beautiful woman, *and Putney!!!!* she habited in a cowboy costume, as they were going on to the Three Arts Ball! – I sat next to her and got on admirably with her – even to helping arrange her costume!!! – I could have died of laughter tho' to see Herbert and Tommy, Putney and I all gathered together at one board!!!! – if they had only all known everything!! – ye gods and little fishes!! – After it was over about one o'clock – we drove my Lord back to All Souls Place, where he was giving another supper of a domestic nature which he was very insulted that I refused to join!! What rascals men are! . . .

March 20

. . . Next day I went down to see my Lord, and had a few minutes chat in the Dome with him. I told him about the Fez idea [a proposal for Olivia to go to Fez with Mrs Niven, Tommy, and another man whose identity is not clear] which horrified him, as he said that with two men of that sort in the desert, I was bound to be carried away – and if by a miracle I wasn't, everyone would say I had been as their reputations are so moutarde!! – He begged me not to go – and so of course I obeyed! Is it not wonderful the way I give in to his least wish when I am so headstrong with everyone else – It is just the difference between my love for him and for anyone else – passion and affection I have given them, and shall give – but not the sort of blind devotion which makes me sacrifice myself without hope of reward – for of course he won't think any more of me for it – He is too busy to really trouble if I go to Fez or to Hell!

May 11

. . . I went to several plays, of which 'The School for Scandal' was of course the first. It is naturally very inferior to the original production but one is never likely to see a cast like that again – and it was quite fairly acted. One missed dear old Henry Nevill's Sir Oliver the most. Phyllis Terry was much better than I had expected – and looked really handsome – But Herbert never seems to act well with her – he shows his dislike for her personality – the origin of which may be that she makes open fun of him!! – I thought of you – as I have never seen him so knock-kneed! However – he was most sweet and dear to me – coming frequently to the box . . .

May 21

. . . I caught a brief glimpse of Herbert on Monday evening – he came in to the box office and found me talking to Mr Potter – this is the second time this has happened when he didn't know I was in London so he will certainly soon suspect an intrigue there!!! – He was very dear – and tho' worked to death, very well – 'Ariadne in Naxos' is going to be a big show – it costs him £800 a night – and it will take him all his time to get it back without any possibility of making any profit!! – Was ever a man so truly devoted to his art, to stake his fortune and give up his time and energy, just for the love of it!! Even I – have to pay for my seats at the first night as none are to be given away. I look forward to it hugely as I think Herbert has a splendid part and will make a great success. I think I have seldom been more crazy about him – I feel like blowing up with the strength of my feelings for him! – I long to prove it by some act of phenomenal self-sacrifice!! don't mind me!! – but the more I see of him and of other men – the greater do I think him – a giant among pygmies. Burke has finally put his foot in it with me, by writing and saying that 'he hears from all sources that my friend Tree simply cannot keep his hands off a pretty girl

– but suppose I am original enough not to go through the mental and physical massage he deals out'!! – I long to tear my nails down his face – and the faces of all the people who dare say such vile things – but I shall not reply to his letter and give him the satisfaction of knowing that he has got a rise out of me – but he has caught me on the one tender spot and I shall not forget or forgive.

With love,
OMT

Then, ten days later, the first night:

. . . I had front row dress circle seats which did very well as there was quite a different crowd there to usual. Viola was of course present, and so changed by the way she now does her hair that I did not know her. I am afraid the show is not a success. The play is sacrificed entirely to the opera which is so boring – in spite of good music exquisitely sung – that even I could hardly sit thro' it! there is no action at all – only the two chief women expressing their sentiments alternately at interminable length. In the 'Perfect Gentleman' Herbert – made up like nothing on God's earth – is very very clever and amusing – but not quite convincing. His effects are calculated – and not the spontaneous and inevitable expression of himself like in Malvolio – He works from the outside, and not the inside – he and his character are not quite one – like Robertson's Hamlet – you can pick no fault – simply you don't feel it. The Terry girl looked lovely.

I am afraid the silly darling will drop a lot over it, and get no kudos . . .

I did not see my lord this time except to press his hand for a minute after the play . . . I wrote and told him my real opinion of his acting tho' – which as usual he took without any offence – possibly because he thinks it is too silly to merit it! . . .

That spring my mother established herself in a house in Bonchurch in the Isle of Wight. It adjoined the house where Dickens wrote *Great Expectations* and was, at last, a move in the right direction financially as I think it *only* had six bedrooms and a staff of three. In July, Herbert went to Marienbad, little suspecting that it was for the last time.

July 25   Marienbad

My dear Olivia,

Thank you for your delightful letter which made me very happy. I hope you will have a lovely time in Jersey where I don't think I have ever been. Yes I am quite alone and trying to work though I feel rather lazy up till now, but I am wonderfully well and hoarding up powder for the coming campaign. I thought I gave you the book [Tree's own *Thoughts and After-Thoughts*], but I will have a nice one sent you. I had given orders to have a vellum copy for you – and will put an inscription on the front page. I am happy to say the book is a really big success. I was overcome by T.P's more than generous notice. I haven't seen 'Punch', but one is bound to get some knocks. I could have written a severe skit myself, but as you say, it is pleasant that the people should know what one really feels about things . . .

Not many English people here but such as are, are very hospitable to me. I expect May will come out for the last few days – she loves Marienbad more than any place in the world and she has so little of life that this is a real treat to her. Claude is still in London and will, I think, join Irving.

Yes, I wish you could come here one year, when I can afford it, I must ask a kind of house-party here. It is so lovely and restful. When do you return to London? I hope you will be at our first night.

I have no great news from England – Viola and Felicity and Iris are going to a little house we have taken in France and I daresay I shall join them for a few days before returning to London. Max is still Rapalloing – what a wonderful, peaceful life he has – none of the storm and stress and anguish of things.

Do write me another sweet letter. Have you a copy of my book? – if not I will at once ask them to send you one. Thank you for all your goodness to me and your encouragement. I do hope you will soon meet with someone whom you can love and respect enough to marry.

Believe me ever yours affectionately,
Herbert

In August Olivia is privileged to observe a rehearsal of Tree's production of Joseph.

. . . and afterwards I went down to *the* rehearsal at *the* theatre! – Herbert – just returned and in wonderful health – and Parker were conducting it from a scaffolding facing the stage on which the cast in street costume were squatting whilst a pale young man in spectacles declaimed over a dirty rag representing Joseph's coat of many colors!! I wanted to roar with laughter until my lord stepped down and showed everybody how to do everything including an eastern dance!! – his imagination and personality dominated it all so completely as to entirely carry one away – it was the most amazing example of his power I have ever seen – and held me spellbound. I think it is going to be a great show – and a sure draw – I only wish I could get to the first night. I had hoped my dear one would let me dine with him – but he had to attend to another old love who was just leaving for America! – however he came round to the hotel about ten o'clock and was very nice to me – and I was very pleased and flattered . . .

His usual robust health deserted him a little that winter, and caused me anxiety – I think I suggested some sort of thought-healing treatment to help his vitality, but the idea does not seem to have appealed to him.

Friday   His Majesty's Theatre

My dear Olivia,

    I am dreadfully sorry not to have seen more of you – but I have been really ill all the week.

    The night you saw me I was asked to sup and couldn't – I am unfit for human food just now. Let me know how much longer you are in town. Ring me up to-morrow (Saturday).

    I am quite weak with my coughs and paroxysms.

                                      Ever yours, H

My dear Olivia,

    It is too good of you to take so much trouble and to care so much. But no one can do me any good by that sort of influence – it would make me laugh – my vitality is all right – and I shall soon be quite myself again. I tried to get back the other day and couldn't. I had promised poor Claude Lowther to sit with him and this I had to forgo too.

Then came the beginning of a closer relationship with Herbert's mistress, May Reed.

                                          The Stanhope Hotel,
October 7   Stanhope Gardens, Queen's Gate, S.W.

. . . On Monday Mother comes up and I join her at the Rembrandt Hotel for a fortnight – I have been to two plays so far – the celebrated 'Hindle

Wakes' which is very good – and Shaw's 'Androcles and the Lion' most of which with its clever skit of modern christians – and its profound sense of real religion, delighted me – tho' I am sure it bores most people stiff – The man who does the lion is a genius.

On Saturday afternoon I went down to Ranelagh with Beatrice [sister of Olivia's ex-fiancé Oliver Valpy, and later her daughter Isolde's godmother] to play golf – and from there went on to see Herbert's lady!!!! – I cannot describe to you the mixed feelings with which I waited on that doorstep, across which for so many years I have watched my beloved one disappearing into her arms!! – It is a curious house all on one floor with very large, rather mysterious rooms opening out of each other divided by curtains – and intensely quiet – except for the children's voices – his children!! – The lady herself was extremely nice to me – hers is a very vivid and arresting personality – pagan in its intensity of passion – she did nearly all the talking – and I listened fascinated. She told me a long story of some people who are trying to blackmail Herbert on her account – most disgraceful – and he has displayed his very worst qualities of weakness and indecision. I believe she could kill a person – even Herbert – very easily – and yet she has amazing dignity and breadth of character – curiously honest – and yet very femine – a woman of breeding too. I quite understand how she has dominated him all this time. She showed me the pictures of their children – besides Claude 3 boys and a girl! – beautiful creatures – again proving the eugenic theory! I stayed a long time – and when I left arranged to dine with her to-morrow night!!! – I am sure I am foolish – as she could turn me inside out with the greatest ease – but glamour of mystery – of being his loved one – and her own charm – are irresistable to me. It is not easy for me to see her – as I don't want Wiltshire the lynx eyed to know – she would not understand at all – to her of course wedlock is propriety – whereas this woman has led a life of almost austere devotion and virtue! – I have done more wrong than she – How queer – how very interesting life is! – To-night I hope to go to 'Joseph' and to supper with Herbert! . . .

The next letter comes from Dorset where Olivia was staying with a friend.

November 3   Chantmarle, Dorchester

. . . I went that day to lunch with May – I had very little private talk with her as Claude was there all the time – but I gathered that at the time Herbert used to come to Landford and be dropped by her in the road – I used to cause her no little anxiety! The children were *all* produced for me to inspect – 5 of them – all quite charming especially the small girl – they certainly did harrow my feelings too dreadfully – why should she have so many and I none! – If I don't marry I shall try and get her to let me adopt one – at any rate it would be part of my dear lord! . . . Next night I went to see Claude act – which he did very well in quite the rottenest play imaginable. Different inherited mannerisms quite fascinated me! – He was by way of coming back to supper with me – and incidentally Cockie Alexander at Billy's rooms – but had a row with his father over my tickets, and never turned up – however what was much more important his father *did*!! The night before he had been so cross to me down the telephone that I could have killed him for it – and spent hours weeping helplessly on the floor in the dark – but he had quite recovered and was charming – He read us a new short story that he had written – and then about 1.15 I motored him and his bag out to Putney – and saw him disappear to the connubial couche!!! What a situation!

I think I have at last grown to love him quite selflessly – I have conquered all my revolting pride. I know that honor binds him to her – that I can have no active place in his life – and yet I believe as firmly as ever that he is and must be mine – if only I have the strength and the patience to expiate whatever I must formally have done wrong – by resisting any carnal union with him this incarnation – He has yet to learn to controle himself – and to love spiritually – and I have the curious psychic knowledge – or delusion – that the first steps of his advancement or retrogression lie with me – and my power to resist – do you laugh at this? . . .

Next there seems to have been a very slight and unusual jar between us. I believe he sent a better bound copy of the book he had just published to a royalty than he did to me!

December 11

My dear,

I am terribly sorry to have been so remiss in answering your kind letter, but indeed I have not been in the mood to do anything charming. My health is for the moment suffering eclipse. I don't write any letters when I am in this mood – not even to Kings and Chancellors!

By the bye, there is often a touch of east-wind about your amiability. As for being 'snobby', it leaves me quite unscathed. It so happens that for days I have vainly been trying to write an important letter to a royalty – a minor one – it is true!

I am sorry I ordered that specially bound copy of my book for the old Queen, if it annoys you, – but is not this natural? I wrote a grateful little inscription – and it pleased her, no doubt. *You* are pleased with the contents – a different thing.

I will let you know all about birthday and other arrangements on Monday – I am afraid you won't be here for Xmas – I am very sorry.

I send this in the hope it may still reach you to-morrow.

Ever yours,

H

Olivia's last two letters of 1913 recount her quarrel and reconciliation with Herbert.

. . . In that condition [she had toothache] I went to lunch with Claude – who looked very peaky and unwholesome – and was full of grumbles about Herbert – whose temper he says is dreadful – Afterwards I met Beatrice at the Leicester Gallery where there was a charming exhibition including some of Dulac's – and we went on to see my Lord whom we found 'sitting' in the dome to a Mrs Cotton to whom I took an instant dislike – she went away – and he occupied himself signing a copy of his book for Queen Alexandra – much better bound than mine which made me furious, as I should never dream of giving some miserable royalty anything better than I gave him! – He was very tired and cross – and stood about spitting with rage like an old goose on a green!! – I am sure he makes more love than is good for him – and uses all his vitality – I want him to see a quack man of Minnie's who has 'vital energy' – it might be just the thing.

. . . Sunday I lunched with Mrs Bristowe – and by so doing missed my beloved who came to see me at 3.30! – he will do it without warning me – if I wait in he doesn't come – quoi faire?! Of course I was in despair . . .

Olivia now left for a short ski-ing holiday in Switzerland prior to her trip to Egypt as a guest of Harry Uniacke and his wife. The surprising reappearance of her Tasmanian admirer, Nikola, is explained by the arrival in England of his regiment. His father's obdurate refusal to increase his meagre allowance and so make marriage possible accounts for his long silence. It is evident that Olivia, as usual, remained on friendly terms with her former admirer.

Hotel Alpina,
Gstaad, Berner-Oberland

Xmas Day 1913

. . . In the evening I took the Bristowes – with whom I was staying – to see 'Joseph' – and Nikola joined us there coming up from Norwich after shooting – missing his dinner and changing in the train – so I was very flattered! I liked the play better than ever – It grows on one – I saw Herbert – and he was quite horrid to me – because in despair at not getting an answer out of him about my quack doctor – I wrote and accused him of being a snob!! my ruse succeeded so well that he answered at once!! – but he took it quite seriously which was absurd of him! I nearly burst into tears – but was afraid of annoying him more – He waved me to a distant chair and glowered at me! – I tried to drown my despair in champagne at the Carlton . . . I forgot to say Max was in the theatre – with his wife – a less dreadful looking person than I expected – He looks very middle aged and rangé!!

. . . I struggled out to dinner with Mother and Ivor [Olivia's eldest brother] – and went on to the revue at the Alhambra which is certainly excellent. At the end we called round to see Herbert – and offer birthday congratulations in person – This time he was more gracious – and our reconciliation was completed when he turned up at Victoria next morning to see me off! . . . I had very few words with either him or Mother – but publicly embraced him with much fervor!! Mother tells me that he was almost moved to tears! . . .

So the last year before the Great War ended in harmony with the following letter from Herbert:

December 29   Garrick Club

My dear Olivia,

How lovely your description of your abode sounds. I would I were there too. Don't think I do not value all your goodness to me – only I was hurt at your little sneer (as it seemed to me). The ivory brush is lovely indeed. I am sending you a present – you will receive it on New Year's Day, I hope.

I drove all round the town yesterday, trying to find something nice – but couldn't. The best shops were shut up, but I hope to be fortunate to-morrow. I went away to join the family at Belvoir – but came up again on Christmas Day to amuse the children at May's. It was very lovely.

To-night (Sunday) I have to go to Manchester by the midnight train – to see a piece by a friend. I am entertained by the Lord Mayor at lunch and return to London in time for 'Jacob' to-morrow night. If that is not energy, I don't know what is!

Viola is very happy and looks forward to her new motherhood in February.

I wish you a very very happy and eventful New Year, and every blessing that can be bestowed on you . . .

Yours affectionately,
Herbert

1914 – 1917

After the short holiday in Switzerland Olivia went as planned to spend the early months of 1914 with the Uniackes in Egypt, and to disguise her affaire with the Colonel, was usually escorted by two other young men, to one of whom, Charles Mackintosh, she then became engaged.

And so back to England and to Herbert, having more or less promised to marry Charles! Looking back, I am totally unable to understand what possessed me to behave in this extraordinary fashion. Charles was an intellectual young man with a strong sense of humour, who wrote long brilliant letters of devotion, but he was no Adonis and had very little money. He had been brought up by two maiden aunts in South Kensington, and, in spite of Eton, rather showed it. I was not in love with him – how could I be with Herbert as the *leit motif* and Harry as a variation! Herbert had certainly for a long while been urging me to 'commit matrimony', but at twenty-six my case was not yet desperate – I can find no extenuation at all for my conduct. In due course Charles followed me back, and to Bonchurch, where, having come to my senses, I had the unpleasant task of informing him that the engagement was off. To my horror he burst into tears and went on crying uncontrollably. I had never seen a man do that. I was shocked to the core, and had no idea what to say to comfort him. After he left his misery turned to rage to an extent that even killed his sense of humour. He accused me of being a modern Messalina. This seemed a particularly inept comparison; however many pretenders had attached themselves to me, we had never indulged in orgies, nor do I think that Messalina was particularly interested in matrimony. Like all the rest before long he married someone else, I believe quite successfully.

One result of the abortive flirtation with the politician Tommy Platt was my introduction to Sir Edward Carson. Tommy was a very intimate friend of his, and had no liking for the lady to whom he was then paying his addresses. He thought of me as a possible rival, and I was not loth to meet the great

127

lawyer and the head of the Ulster Covenanters, who were sworn to resist to the death their separation from England. I duly signed the Covenant oath, and tried unsuccessfully to present Carson with a bouquet of orange lilies when he was leaving Buckingham Palace after an historic interview with the King. My chances of capturing his fancy, and Ulster's embarking on civil war, were both brought to a sudden end, in the one case by his marrying Ruby Frewen, and in the other by the Kaiser invading Belgium. I retain his signed photo and the memory of his entrancing brogue.

Beyond my making a few speeches on behalf of the Ulster Convenanters – this in spite of Carson being now out of my reach – the early summer passed peacefully and pleasantly enough. In August Harry and his wife were coming on from Cowes to stay with us, and I was of course greatly looking forward to this. Suddenly, without warning, the storm that was to sweep away one's world broke. The Archduke was assassinated, the Austrians declared war, the Germans mobilised, the Russians followed, and we stood on the brink. Herbert was present in the House when the Foreign Minister, Grey, made one of the great speeches of history. Herbert wrote to me as follows – what 'good time' he thought I was having, or was likely to have, I cannot imagine.

July 4 [actually August 4]   His Majesty's Theatre

My dear,

I am writing this from the theatre. I daresay you will understand that I have many things to do.

Yes, it is an appalling time; I was in the House yesterday when Grey and Redmond made their great speeches – it was the most impressive thing I have ever seen.

I think the Germans have 'bitten off more than they can chew', for once – I imagine – however, that the first victories may be with them.

I am worn out with the excitement of it and hope to get away alone somewhere to work. I think you had better send any letters to the Garrick. I will ask them to forward them. I fear there is not much chance at present of my getting to you – but I will try to manage it.

I hope you are having a good time. I fear we are in for a ruinous season in the theatres owing to the war, but others have great suffering and it is easy to be philosophical about oneself when one can sympathise with others.

I am worried to think there is any new gossip about me, only this I know that I have done nothing to incur it, – but people will never be happy unless they are making others unhappy with their tongues. Perhaps you

will allay the chatter by saying that I lead a very quiet sort of life – indeed
my work would preclude any other sort of existence . . .

Yours devotedly,
H

*Then two short references from Olivia to Herbert and his doings in letters of July
20th and August 27th.*

. . . Herbert is keeping 'Pygmalion' on until the end of this week – so if you
would like to see it on Wednesday afternoon – I can easily arrange it – only
I don't think I will go with you as I have seen it *so* often . . .

. . . I suppose you saw that quite contrary to my expectations – Herbert
has turned out a very fine Drake – I always thought him merely a duck!! – I
long to run up and see him, before I am tied down to nursing for an
indefinite period – but do not know whether I ought to spend the money on
a purely personal pleasure –

*After seeing Harry Uniacke and her beloved brother Billy off to the war, Olivia
continues:*

After my excursion to Lyndhurst I found that I could bear the inactivity at
Bonchurch no longer. I announced my intention of going to work in London,
and as usual got my own way. Before long I was living in a block of newly built
flats in Shepherd's Market; I was one of the first occupiers, to be shortly
followed by half the population of what were then referred to as 'ladies of
pleasure'. I shall always regret that I did not keep a diary of the goings on
there, which were of the most lurid kind – the comings and goings of lovers, of
enraged wives, and loud quarrels – even, I think, a suicide, though we
stopped short of a murder. Here of course came Herbert to see me – that I saw
him frequently is evidenced by the following undated note:

Tuesday night   1 All Souls Place, Portland Place

My dear Olivia,
        I am sorry it was impossible to get to you to-day. I hope you may
look me up to-morrow (Wednesday). Do tell me what you are going to do
with yourself.
        What a time we live in – it is too appalling to think of all the suffering, of

all the horrors – a hundred years of ease cannot compensate for one week of war. *This must be the last!*

Blessed is the anarchist that shall rid humanity of its monarchs whose vanity plunges humanity in misery. But this, I suppose, is not the moment to talk of Christianity.

Of course I shall keep my courage. I shall probably go to America to make money for mine.

Best love, Your devoted.
H.B.T.

Olivia gives Miss Mackay news of Charles Mackintosh's letter of abuse to her, the death in hospital of Oliver Valpy, her relief at having Harry back safely in hospital with a head wound which was not serious, together with details of the work she was undertaking, and then refers again to Herbert in this letter of November 28th.

. . . Have I seen you since the first night of 'Henry IV' – I expected to be bored, but it is a lovely production – *so* well acted – Matheson Lang a wonderful Hotspur – Gill an ideal King – and my lord of course inimitable as Falstaff . . .

Then from Billy's rooms in Sloane Street on December 12th:

. . . Sunday my lord brought May to dine at Sloane Street!! such a funny little party! – He was very peaceful and nice but not as amusing as usual – she, I think, felt her posistion, and was rather jumpy and unnatural . . . Fourteen years ago, when to breathe the same air as he did seemed too great joy – if I could have looked into the future and seen that evening what would my feelings have been! – The utter strangeness of life – and its terrible humour behind all the pain! . . . One night I went to see a very beautiful exhibition of skating at Princes in aid of the Relief Fund – my friend Grenander was there and fairly excelled himself – [Henning Grenander was a Swedish skater, and protégé of the Duchess of Westminster, whom Olivia had met and admired in Switzerland.]

I took Harry and his wife to 'Drake' and 'Henry IV' – the latter of which I enjoyed more than ever – it is a shame the public not liking it – as Herbert says – they only care to see a man being sick in a hat! . . .

A very sweet incident was that the Tommies to whom I have been teaching French – 3 of whom are just off to the front – have clubed together and given me an inkstand! – I do think it too darling of them don't you –

and such a feather in my cap! The lower orders always love me which shows that I must have something good at bottom! . . .

And from Bonchurch on December 23rd:

. . . all my best love and wishes for Xmas – I hope that it may be a peaceful one – more one cannot hope this tragic year . . .

But in March 1915 Harry was killed. Olivia continues:

Actually it was the cutting of the Gordian Knot. The future held nothing for our relationship. Under no circumstances would Harry ever have left his wife, and his retirement would probably have taken them to Scotland – he was not a London man. Matrimony, for me, would have remained still uncommitted, with very little in return for the sacrifice. Into this vacuum in my life which left me unhappy and lonely stepped Cyril [Cyril Wigram, her first admirer when she lived at Landford], on the eve of joining the Flying Corps, his revived ardour as great as ever. With what proved absurd Quixotism, I thought it would be fine to bring joy to at least one person, even if I got little myself – a person moreover who had all the odds against him of survival. I promised to marry him as soon as his divorce proceedings were complete, and from then on saw as much of him as circumstances permitted.

My memory of the fearful years that followed is confused. I engaged in so many jobs, and met so many people. One of the first jobs was taking round weekly allowances from the S.S.A.F.A.* to the dependants of soldiers who had not yet received their pension cards, and were in pressing need. Personally I have always bitterly resented unbidden strangers breaking in on me, and have the greatest reluctance in breaking in on them. However on the whole I succeeded in my task, and was made welcome in a number of homes. It was my first encounter with real poverty in the pre-Welfare State – the under-nourished children, the penury which doomed old people to lie in pain because they could not afford even a little aspirin, the squalor in the case of sluttish housewives, above all the smell of the unwashed, which greeted one with such force as to make one stagger in the doorway, struggling against vomiting – brought me down at last out of my cloud-cuckoo land.

My brother, who had eventually managed to rejoin his regiment, came home on leave and stayed in the flat adjoining mine, which Wiltshire had

* That same charity for which she first wrote to Tree, as a child of twelve, to solicit a contribution – and a letter.

occupied till then. He was horrified at my surroundings and the character of the inhabitants, and insisted on my leaving. So that the following year found me in a dear little eighteenth-century house in Derby Street, Mayfair. The ground floor was occupied by a dairy, but the noise of the milk churns in the early hours was considered preferable to that of their clients leaving the ladies of the town.

In further letters that spring, after detailing the different work she was doing, including the supply of comforts to the Gordon Highlanders with Harry's wife, Olivia goes on to refer to Herbert:

February 7   27 Carrington Court, Mayfair

. . . I haven't been to any other theatre, except 'Copperfield' again – when Herbert's wonderful acting impressed me more than ever. He drove me home afterwards – sat for 10 minutes with his head quietly on my shoulder, and then wandered out again!! He was fearfully anxious to know whether he was the first person to kiss me in this room – which was rather a leading question!! – May and I appeared together at a slum club entertainment the other night – which was not without humour I think! . . .

Sunday, May 16   27 Carrington Court, Mayfair

. . . Nor have I told you about Herbert's new play. It was a delightful first night with heaps of interesting people there . . . The play is good, but not excellent – and Herbert acts with much charm in it – but he will never stand out in a modern part . . . I have not seen Herbert, who has had gout and been very depressed about it, but May came to tea with me last week – and told me that he has taken on Lady Townsend to read plays for him and that she stays in the dome with him half the night!! It is too absurd of him . . .

There were to be very few more letters from Herbert, but the following one came in July.

July 21   Royal Hotel & Baths, Matlock-Bath

Yes, here I am. I had intended to ring you up before leaving but there was, as you may imagine, a rush of things. I have been working fairly well down here. May and Guy [one of May Reed's five sons by Tree] have now come – it would have been jolly if you could have come. I return to London on Sunday evening, and shall then be preparing for Henry VIII at H.M. and Trilby in the Variety Theatres. It is useless to attempt any serious work at my theatre – the public only want funny things. It is lamentable, mais c'est la guerre!

I suppose most of us will have to begin life again after the war.

I hope you will continue to have good news from your brother. I fear the Russians are in a bad way just now and this may have a bad effect upon the general face of the war.

I am going to deliver an address on the war at Queen's Hall on the 8th July. It is indeed a sad time we have to endure. Perhaps we have laughed at the Devil too long and he is asserting himself with a vengeance.

How good of you to work so hard for the poor soldiers. You will always feel glad through your life that you have helped. I hope your friend is wrong about my being unbearable in success. I always feel it makes me very modest – but in failure I feel a fine conceit that helps me through.

It is quite lovely here and I think I am getting health. I haven't been quite happy about myself lately. May was glad to see you the other day – we must arrange a little meeting next week.

Take great care of your precious self.

Good-bye, dear Olivia. Thank you for all your sweetness to me, and believe ever

Your devoted,
H

'I must have been seeing him till the time he went to America in 1915,' continues Olivia whom we interrupt here to insert this description of Tree's departure. The Potter incident relates to Tree's dismissal of his box-office manager whom, in the interests of economy, he replaced with a woman. Happily, he had second thoughts and eventually took him on again, though it is not clear if he was influenced by Olivia's pleas. This letter to Miss Mackay was written on November 15th 'on the train'.

. . . On Thursday Herbert took his departure for America – May very kindly asked me out to meet him at her house on Sunday for tea – after which he drove me up to town – The scene at the station was diverting in the extreme – There he stood surrounded by duchesses – playwrights – actors – cameras – wives – children – grandchildren – orchids – luggage and imprecations! shaking hands with impartial vagueness and courtesy – I feel that his going marks the end of a period in our long association – for I shall never quite forgive him his treatment of poor Potter – to whom he has not only shown the rankest ingratitude but whom he has even done out of £5 – !! – And this after I had made the matter a personal one – which shows that his regard for me is of the slightest – They tell me that he generally tires thus of old servants – and a more objectionable trait I cannot imagine – alas! indeed has every human divinity the feet of clay – and perhaps I love Harry the better and more truly because I had no illusions about him! It has hurt me horribly and made me feel very unhappy . . .

Life in London was not as disrupted as it became in the 1939 war – we had bombs, but I never realised how many till I saw a map of them recently, and I expect people bored one about *their* bomb as much as they did later.

Other jobs turned up. I went to work in a canteen in an Acton factory, where a very young man came regularly to eye me soulfully, and at length plucked up courage to ask me to go for a row with him on the Serpentine! I always wish that I had gone.

The war ran its dreadful course, with ever-mounting casualties till most of the men one had met had appeared in the lists of dead, wounded or missing. Constantly one was going to Victoria to see someone off, including my beloved brother. We were a company of heart-racked women, trying to keep smiling faces to the last, when the train went out carrying its load back to the shambles and horror of the trenches, whilst incompetent generals wrangled with incompetent Ministers. Cyril went overseas and dropped his quota of bombs, surprisingly receiving no injury when a shell went through the rear of his plane. He was one of the few 1915 pilots who survived.

I had now started on a new enterprise. My singing friend, Alys Bateman, organised a concert party to go round camps and hospitals, and I was included in it to give patriotic recitations. Then I wrote two sketches, one or other of which was added to our programme. 'Back from the Trenches' dealt with two old ladies taken in by a bogus soldier, and absolutely brought the house down whenever we gave it. The other sketch was about a publicity-minded duchess who contrived to get all the credit for the war work done by a friend. Viola Tree did the duchess, I did the friend, and old Rutland Barrington of Gilbert and Sullivan fame was also in it, though he never remembered a word of his part.

In 1915, with the death struggle of the nations still showing no sign of coming to an end, Herbert went to America as he had announced, eloquently pleading our cause, whilst playing in a very bad film of *Macbeth*. From New York, that next spring, he wrote to me.

16 March 1916   New York

My dear Olivia,

Thank you for your sweet letters and for all your kind and womanly thoughts. Time is flying – and here I am back in New York. We have had an enormous success with Henry VIII – it looks as if I had a real hold over the New York public – that will be a great income in the future – for I am only anxious during these days to reap a harvest and then retire – to eternity. Iris has stayed behind with friends in California; but she rejoins me to-morrow. I am delighted you have seen May and the children – do cheer her up – she seemed rather depressed at times, and full of morbid imaginings – surely she has no grounds for being unhappy on my account. I am glad you like Juliet [Tree's only daughter by May Reed] – she is indeed a gracious little creature. I am tremendously excited every morning about the war news – really it looks as if Germany were spending her force in the West – but to-morrow I suppose we shall know the result of Verdun.

Do forgive me for not writing oftener, but I have not had time for writing – in California I frequently worked 18 hours a day and was getting quite ill from fatigue – I lost twelve pounds in weight.

And how are you? – I hope *your* shadow is no less!

Good-bye, dear.

Ever your affectionate,
Herbert

How strange that he should talk of reaping a rich harvest and then retiring to eternity – which is exactly what he did. *Chu Chin Chow* was having its long run at His Majesty's, and from it he had royalties. Every soldier on leave went to see it, its brilliant colours contrasting so greatly with the mud and squalor from which they came, its catchy tunes accompanying them back to the battlefields, the memory of its beauty perhaps blotting out some of the ghastly sights with which they had to live.

Olivia describes the day out with May referred to in Herbert's letter:

. . . This afternoon I took May and the 3 boys to the submarine picture at the Philharmonic!! A quite interesting and very wonderful show which I think they enjoyed – poor thing it is miserable for her with Herbert away – He nearly got dreadfully had in New York as when he got over there, he found the film company was more or less bogus – but tho' he was there all alone – he managed to get a new contract at the same salary – and so has come out top – He is not such a fool as he pretends by a long way! He won't be back before November anyhow. I found his pictures on one of my Clapham women's table yesterday – I told her I knew him 'He calls 'isself an *actor* don't 'e?' – she enquired!!! I ventured to remark that I thought he might make some small claim to the title!! – bless him! . . .

Still in the States, working on the film of Macbeth, *Tree wrote to Olivia from California on the 22nd July, and there is a further reference to Olivia's baritone friend Edmund Burke.*

My very dear Olivia,

Thank you for your letter – which has been most interesting reading. Everything seems to be moving in the right direction.

I do hope your brother in Mesopotamia is quite safe now. Geoffrey Cory-Wright (Felicity's husband) is out there too. Felicity [Tree's second daughter] is to have a baby (D.V.) in August. I cannot tell you in words how deep was my disappointment in not crossing – I wanted to see you all – and I wanted to be in the danger zone. Here everything is quite peaceful – and indecently prosperous.

I was really rather 'run down' – but I am wonderfully recovered.

The days and nights are exquisite climatically. I thought the Macbeth film remarkably good – but of course the wondrous words are mourned. I am glad you have seen dear May – she is always in my thoughts – I wish you could bring her over here – you would both love it. How fine for your big brother to have got the command of his old regiment – they seem to be using the cavalry now. Claude is joining the Canadian Army – I am so glad.

It is news to me about Beecham! He is a remarkable person – full of talent but lacking in character.

I see Burke is still on the tapis – or at least on the doormat. I have nearly finished my story 'Nothing Matters' – good, I think. I have loads of letters to write – so pray accept these scraps.

With love believe me always,
Herbert

One sentence in Herbert's letter causes one to smile today, that 'Beecham is a remarkable person, full of talent but lacking in character'! Tommy Beecham, who has proved one of the outstanding characters of our time.

Tree was on a brief visit to England, and Olivia heard about it while staying with her mother at Bonchurch.

September 23   4 Derby Street, Mayfair

. . . but suddenly discovered that Herbert had been home nearly a week, and as he was only staying about a fortnight I hurried back to London to catch him. He came to see me one day at tea time, sat down on the sofa, and went sound asleep! – He brought me nothing back from America – did not seem the least pleased to see me, and has departed again without troubling about me any further! I suppose he has given up all hope of me! . . .

But he wrote from America again:

October 18   Boston, Massachusetts

My dearest Olivia,
    I am very sorry indeed to have missed you before leaving London. Thank you for writing to me so sweetly.
    I stayed in New York till last week – then came on here with Iris. Boston is not a very fascinating place from any point of view. I think we shall hardly be the same success here as at New York.
    By the bye you must get the money for the dog-collar from May – I will ask her to pay it to you. I am glad you saw her – she is very sweet but has had a hard time and she is a little variable on that account. I hope she may be coming out – there is a chance of her doing so. But I hope to be back myself at the end of January – we might make an expedition together.
    The theatre is going on splendidly I am glad to say, and much of my anxiety is thus lifted from my mind.
    I hope to be doing useful work here, talking to the people. I suppose you are as busy as ever with all your soldier work. I hope your brothers will both be all right.
    Here they say that there has been a most disastrous air-raid over London – but it is from a German source and is no doubt made to console them for the loss of the Zepps.
    Write and tell me how you are and what you are doing.
    Take great care of yourself, dear, won't you. Oh, I wish all were settled and that we could meet without these terrible fears.
                     Ever yours devotedly,
                     Herbert B. Tree

They were the final words he penned to me.

In the spring of 1917 Herbert returned from America; *Chu Chin Chow* was in full spate, and he never appeared in his beloved theatre again. I think it was while Cyril was confined to barracks after being court-martialled for appropriating used aircraft fuel that Herbert, who had presumably made a tour of his new grandchildren, took May for a holiday to Broadstairs. Whilst there he slipped on some steps and injured his kneecap – it did not seem serious, but when May went to help him up he said, with sudden prophecy, 'This is the end.'

He was taken to a London nursing home and operated on by Sir Alfred Fripp, who had patched up Maud's jaw. His progress after the operation seemed perfectly normal. I went to see him, taking him a big bunch of St Joseph lilies and delphiniums, flowers which I now always associate with his passing. He was in good spirits, revising a book he had written and full of plans for the future – the idea of film production had bitten him.

Olivia reported her last sight of Tree to Miss Mackay in a letter from Derby Street dated June 23rd.

. . . You have of course seen about Herberts accident . . . I have seen him once since he has been in hospital – looking very squelchy – with his hair on end – and quite unattractive pyjamas – Poor old darling! – I have just read his book which is really brilliantly clever – He is a wonderful man . . .

We parted with the utmost affection and I went back to Bonchurch, where I was joined by Cyril on his release from his imprisonment. Walking through the village with him, the man I was to marry, I thought I would but a newspaper at the shop. They only had the *Daily Express* which prints its leading news on the outside sheet. I took one up and went out into the road. My eye fell on the lines 'Sudden Death of Sir Herbert Tree' – and the whole world ceased to matter.

Years previously in rather a poor play about a desert island he had had to die one of his many deaths – but on that occasion he imparted something so real to it that I was appalled. I looked over into the abyss which his real going would create – I was so overcome that I could not speak long after the performance was ended and I was with him in the royal room. Now the abyss was there in fact, and not in pretence.

At last Olivia recovered enough to write to Miss Mackay:

July 11   4, Derby Street, Curzon Street

Dearest Aunt Judy,

Forgive my interminable silence but I have felt unable to write – even to you. The shock was so utterly dreadful – I saw him two days before I left London looking too comic bless him, with his hair brushed forward a la Romaine – a yellow scarf round his neck – and a purple and gold bed cover – I cannot *now* realise that one will never see him act again. His loss to the stage is measureless – no one approaches him in any way – he was one of the great personalities of the time in spite of his weaknesses and absurdities –

To me of course it is irreparable – He has dominated my whole life and I owe him more than I could ever repay – There must be some link even stronger than that of affection between us – because his going leaves me with a sense of something broken – an essential factor gone which I did not get even with Harry – I can't say that I really wish him back – Anyone is lucky to have done with the world today, and he has died the death that he would have given thousands to die – he feared it so much – and it came in an instant without even a spasm. May was with him only half an hour before – and his last words were of her. He said to the nurse 'She is a *wonderful* woman' then 'She is a marvellous mother' then 'She is a noble woman. She makes one feel – happy!'

Isn't it a lovely help for her. I cannot tell you how fine and brave and dignified she is – I admire her infinitely – Thank goodness he has left her the half of everything, and that he has left a good deal of money. Lady Tree has behaved with inconceivable vulgarity – No doubt you saw the picture of her in exaggerated weeds sprawling over his grave – She also dressed herself in black went to bed covered by his pall, and received her friends thus! How disgusted and contemptuous he must feel. The memorial service was fearful. The Bishop pronounced unctuous platitudes in a sonorous voice – and Clara Butt bellowed forth a solo. Most people came to see who else was there – and made a hateful atmosphere. I sat in the same pew as Mr Potter, who felt it quite amazingly – he and I perhaps loved him more than anyone else there . . .

Forgive this terribly egoistic letter – I have just been to see Potter and Dana at His Majesty's – and it brings it home to one so cruelly –

With best love,
Olivia

I attended his memorial service at St Martin's-in-the-Fields, sitting in the pew with his box-office manager, who had served him long and faithfully. Because he loved him also, I think he knew a little of what I felt, whilst the worthy bishop made platitudes which would have bored Herbert, and the large congregation of celebrities, experts at memorial services, sighed the sighs proper to the occasion. He was cremated, and his ashes buried at Hampstead. One cannot connect that radiant personality with *pompes funèbres*. Round my neck I wear the only bit of his earthly body which survives – a lock of hair I cut from his head, the while he was nonchalantly reading a newspaper.

Within a little while his beloved theatre had passed into the hands of the philistines, and all his personal treasures had been put up to public auction. I was present at the sale and watched them go one by one: the oil paintings of him in various of his roles; the furniture from the dome – even my small presents: the brick from Nero's statue I had brought him from Rome when he was acting the play of that name, and had had mounted with a piece of Antony's rostrum as an antique lamp; the gold-mounted notebook he carried; the very frame that used to hold my photo. In the dusty auction room among the Jews and dealers, Viola and I sat in a grief too deep for tears.

Life without Herbert seemed almost inconceivable – for seventeen years I had loved him, and he had been the pivot of my existence. With the exception of Harry, my other distractions had been relatively unimportant. Occult students differentiate the 'personality' and the 'individual'. The 'persona' – the Latin for 'mask' – represents the transient embodiment: the 'individual' is the eternal 'I am'. With my persona I had played on the shores of life with other personas who would pass on their way – Herbert was the friend of my soul, I hope I can say 'is'. In spite of my numerous associations with men, though in a sense I 'love' them, with few exceptions I do not 'like' them. Only Herbert have I worshipped. I wish I had remained entirely his: he who has associated with the King should not dally with the camp followers. Yet he himself never ceased to urge me to marry and not to forego wifehood and motherhood. I should certainly have done better without the former, but I should have missed a wonderful experience without the latter. I have been asked whether I regret the cost of my friendship with the great actor. Most emphatically not. I may have paid for it with my reputation: no one doubted I was his mistress – why should they? – but he taught me the noblest things in life.

Without him I should be quite another person from what I am today. I was born into an environment whose members were narrowly class-conscious, conservative in politics, content to live in luxurious idleness. Theirs not to question why; theirs but to live a lie – the lie of their superior right to the good things of this world. Tree's soul was inspired by the spiritual realities and was nourished on beauty; because I loved him he helped me to escape from the limitations of my class, and to share his ideals and his interests. To him too I owe my love of the theatre and all pertaining to it.

Many celebrities have paid tribute to him, his wit, his charm, his great acting, his splendid productions which were the expression of himself. It became fashionable to accuse him of over-elaboration, of swamping the author with his decor, but to him nothing was good enough for the greatest except the best. As mediaeval peoples expressed their worship of God in building the cathedral masterpieces of architecture and filled them with the richest ornaments they could find to offer, so did Herbert build his stage pictures, neglecting no smallest detail of historic correctness. Percy Macquoid, supreme authority on antique furniture, designed for him, Buchel painted for him, the music was always the best. Nothing cheap or tawdry was ever to be seen in his theatre. The actors who were to become the future stars mostly graduated under his management; in those days plays were not producer-ridden, and the players were allowed to express their own genius, nor had such a thing as the Method been thought of. His casts and his staff all adored him, though he both overworked and often irritated them with his jokes and irresponsibility. In a sense he always remained an amateur. His acting capacity did not include tragedy, though no one had such a power of pathos. Caliban and Shylock brought tears to our eyes. His exit in the Westminster Hall scene of *Richard II* was unforgettable.

In some character roles he will never be equalled: Svengali, Malvolio, Falstaff (even his voice grew fat), Fagin, Micawber, D'Orsay, Wolsey – how marvellous he was in them all! But his Mark Antony, his Ulysses, Macbeth and Othello fell short. His voice was not the perfect vehicle as were those of Waller, Ainley and Gill – the latter I think topped them all – and he had a slightly Teutonic intonation which he must have picked up at Göttingen University and which caused him to pronounce 'and' as 'a-and'.

His appearance, as I said before, was impressive with his height and carriage, though he went off a little about the knees. His blue eyes could be dreamily veiled or flash with the sudden fire which Sargent's portrait of him has caught so well. Normally he had a little trip in his gait, which in a way was an expression of his character. He was often accused of affectation, but no one was more himself – only his self happened to be bizarre, and anything bizarre is suspect to the cut-to-pattern Englishman. Puck and Pan dwelt with Jesus in his soul.

Domestically no doubt he was trying, nevertheless his children adored him. Possibly owing to his Dutch blood he had a queer homely longing to wear carpet slippers and bring the fish home in a flail. I doubt however if his marketing would have been very dependable.

Looking back I know that the only thing in my life I have to be proud of is the homage he paid to me. He treated me, a young girl and totally unimportant, as if I had been a queen. I was too silly and full of myself to realise at the time the honour he did me. I seem even to have ordered him about very impudently. How kind, how courteous, how chivalrous he was can be seen from his letters, but he was always kind and courteous, the expression of a soul which is intrinsically distinguished. The graceful word, the graceful act, came naturally to him. I remember one snowy winter evening when I was driving with him in a taxi to Putney – how often I drove there, but half a log was better than no Tree – we broke down, and had to be helped by a passing beggar. Herbert gave him a tip of his usual generosity. The astonished man with unassumed fervour said 'God bless you, sir' to which Herbert instantly replied 'and you too'. For the underdog he had infinite compassion. 'The rich for the poor, the strong for the weak, that is the higher socialism to which we are all struggling, that is the divine goal of humanity.' They were sublime words, and he lived up to them.

He was at his best at the little suppers which I often shared with him in the dome, the cares of his strenuous life cast off, his brilliant wit, his gift as raconteur at its best. Behind the arras dwelt a large woman who cooked the fattest of quails – a bird one never now sees – which I would consume, accompanied by rare Burgundy from a chalice of pure gold, given him as a presentation.

I see now it was best that he went when he did – an old actor, struggling on with the memories of past triumphs is a pitiful being; he died at the height of his fame. Had he lived, postwar conditions would have been intolerable to him: the greed, the sordidness, the ugliness in all the arts.

One of the last letters in Miss Mackay's collection sums up poignantly Olivia's sense of loss. It was written on January 21st, 1918.

. . . I suppose you saw that His Majesty's was sold for £105,000 – £35,000 more than Herbert paid for it – so he died worth £140,000, and May should get about £2000 a year – and they get a lot, as long as 'Chu Chin Chow' runs which looks like going on for ages. It breaks my heart to think of it really gone – I think I loved every stone of the building as well as he did, poor darling. As time passes, his loss comes more and more home to one – he is so utterly irreplaceable – and of how many humans can that be said – With him seems to have gone a certain glory and glamour, living existence a drabber thing. I dream of him so very, very often – I really believe I gave all my best love to him – Harry was nearer my heart, but he never called forth the ecstasy, the worship, the self-abnegation that Herbert did – I wonder what my past relationship can have been to him – and what my future will be . . .

Epilogue

From the point of view of the reader the rest of the story of Beerbohm Tree's Olivia would be an anti-climax and so it ends here with her marriage to my father, a little over a year after Tree's death. But for those who are curious, it seems only fair to summarise briefly the rest of her story as it is told in the remaining chapters of her autobiography and as I myself remember it:

Her marriage to Cyril unfortunately fared no better than most of her other relations with men, and the divorce which had been foreseen by fortune-tellers even while she was in her teens, duly came to pass. They were both extremely strong-willed and had too little in common for the marriage to have much chance of success. Cyril was sent in 1920 on a mission to Persia, where it was expected that Olivia would be able to join him, but he was re-called before she had a chance to go out. His own letters from Persia are vivid and interesting, especially today. He was discharged from the R.F.C. immediately after the First World War as both superiors and subordinates found him difficult to work with, and after the collapse of the Persian mission he was never able to find a suitable job, and living at home was bound in the circumstances to lead to friction. Matters were not made any easier by Olivia's increasing deafness, and also by the hostility towards Cyril of her faithful attendant, Barbara Wiltshire, who maintained a state of open warfare with him. Olivia never had any ordinary married life at all, but I think Cyril must have been very miserable himself to have treated her so badly.

However she had her daughter – myself – and I feel I must here insert what she wrote in her full autobiography, as I know she would have wanted it. It had never occurred to her that she would not have the son she had set her heart on. She wrote: 'This demonstrates how impossible it is for anyone to judge what is best for them. My despised infant grew up to be far more than a daughter to me – a companion such as few mothers have – sharing all my tastes and interests, and showing an unfailing patience with all my trying

145

peculiarities – balancing my emotionalism with her calm judgement and possessing a brain power and strength of character far exceeding mine. That I should not have welcomed her coming is a matter of deep regret to me, even though I have done my best to make it up to her.'

Alas, she was seeing me through rose-tinted spectacles, my intellect is inferior to hers – mine is only a very average intelligence – while far from being patient I was only too often impatient; the calmness was more usually the result of apathy, and I have no more strength of character than my grandmother, whom I rather resemble. I am after all also my father's daughter, and it was therefore inevitable that things should not always proceed smoothly. Nevertheless, though it was often an explosive relationship, it was a very close one, and we did indeed share the same tastes and interests, thus providing for poor Olivia at last a stable and dependable focus for her love until her death.

The faithful Barbara played a particularly important part in our joint lives after Olivia's divorce from Cyril, when I was just eight, as we then all lived together, for Barbara became my nanny. Miss MacKay (whom I called Kay) also figured benevolently in my childhood. Looking back, Olivia blamed herself bitterly for not making use of her talents for cooking or interior decoration and doing a worth while job. In fact it was probably more of a pity that she did not work at her writing. In 1920 she published her second book, *An A.B.C. of Occultism*, which owing to another publishing mischance did not have the success it might have done. It was republished in the 1960s under the title of *A Simple Guide to Psychic Laws* but again without much success.

During the Second World War I was working in a Government department which was evacuated to Oxford, and Olivia followed and took up various jobs at which she worked far harder than I was called upon to do in mine. She worked long hours at a canteen, and this together with the climate at Oxford at one time quite undermined her health. However it was pleasant for her, when we were on leave, to renew acquaintance with Max Beerbohm, who with his wife Florence returned to this country from their home in Italy and spent the war years at Abinger, near Dorking in Surrey. I can remember some very delightful evenings passed in their company, and even listening to one of Max's famous broadcasts on his own wireless. It was I believe as a result of Olivia's prompting that Max's old university, Oxford, bestowed on him the previously overlooked honorary doctorate of letters, just as she saw to it that a plaque was placed on Tree's old house in Sloane Street. She also kept in touch with Tree's sister Constance, and Max's sisters Agnes and the nun Dora, whose work in the slums Olivia loyally helped. I can remember Sister Dora well, and also meeting Viola Tree who, however, sadly died comparatively young of cancer.

With the end of the war we returned to London, and there followed perhaps the happiest time of the second part of her life, when she worked with her old enthusiasm to further the careers of one or two opera-singer friends. She wrote that she was fortunate with many good friends, and she went to endless trouble for them, believing in R. L. Stephenson's maxim 'My duty to my neighbour is much more nearly expressed by saying I have to make him happy, if I may.' She maintained her interest in the theatre and had two plays produced, one a farce which reached the West End as *The Dish Ran Away* (though this was not her title) and ran to over 200 performances; and the other the first ever stage defence of Richard III, *The Sun of York*, with Leslie French as Richard. This was duly damned by the critics though it had a considerable impact on audiences, and some who saw it still remember it well. We both shared a passionate interest in the rehabilitation of Richard III, and Olivia became the first Librarian of the Richard III Society. She was also devoted to animals and looked back on her hunting days with shame.

When I was about twelve – shortly after my grandmother's death I think – Olivia had suffered the traumatic experience of a mastectomy. Now increasing deafness was also to make life difficult, at least until the appearance of the little transistor hearing aids. However she was very interested in the Church's ministry of healing, and was herself healed of a hiatus hernia by the laying on of hands. Her close association with her beloved brother Billy ended with his marriage in the same year as her own. He and Ivor both farmed in Kenya, and Ivor very rarely came home. They both died of cancer, and Olivia had to cope all alone with Ivor's death in a Swiss clinic. Olivia's heart gave trouble in her last years, and she suffered from cardiac asthma. She had a very bad heart attack about five months before her actual death, and I vividly remember that night, and Olivia in the midst of her attacks of pain, suddenly proclaiming with great energy and, it seemed, some surprise 'I'm going to die'. Somehow to me it seemed a much worse experience than the night when she actually did die, for with all the psychic knowledge she had handed down to me, and the continuous psychic link with Herbert over the years, I could not doubt the joy of their reunion.

As she wrote in a foreword to the original Marienbad draft of her book, addressed to Herbert: 'I have written this little book about you here, as a tribute – a little unimportant tribute to your beloved memory – I shall not see it given to the world, which will possibly not want to read it – but when the day comes perhaps we shall be able to laugh about it together, and drawing a little closer, begin the delightful game of "do you remember?"' She had ended the book with the words: 'The gap he left in my life has never been filled. Nevertheless I had his seal engraved with the device of the dove carrying the oak and olive* leaves, and the motto "J'attends".' The waiting now was over.

Olivia's daughter Isolde

---

* Her baptismal name was in fact Olive, and Tree adopted the symbol of the oak.

Index

Index

26–27; first adult meeting with Tree 30
–31; learns of Tree's second family 33–
34; confesses to her mother 34

1906 describes first night of *Nero* 38;
goes with her mother to Italy 39;
reaction to *Daily Mail* attack on Tree 44;
attends first night of *Colonel Newcome* 46
–48; describes Max's first visit 49–50;
and Tree's first visit to Efford 52–54; as
amateur actress 60–61; sends
photograph of Tree and Max to *Tatler* 59,
64, 67; reaction to Maud Tree's affaire
66–67

1907 moves to Landford Manor 71,
73; publishes novel 78; meets future
husband Cyril 79

1908 and 1909 favoured position at
His Majesty's 85; 21st birthday party 89;
unofficial engagement to Oliver Valpy
90; resents Tree's knighthood 91, 92;
end of engagement 92

1910 and 1911 visit to India 93–95;
unofficial engagement to 'Nikola' 95; ends
it 96; studies singing in Paris 99–102;
and Edmund Burke 99, 100–101, 102
–103, 117–118, 136; meets May Reed
100–102; at Bad Ems for ear treatment
104–105

1912 reaction to Tree's appearance on
music halls 107–109; moves to Eastcourt
House 109; meets next suitor Tommy
Platt 109–110; writes a short play 111

1913 meets Harry Uniacke 115; visits
May Reed 120–121; sees Claude
Beerbohm act 122

1914–1917 visits Uniackes in Egypt
127; becomes unofficially engaged to
Charles Mackintosh 127; and ends it
127; meets Edward Carson 127; moves
to London 129; promises to marry Cyril
131; gives patriotic recitations 134; hears
of Tree's death 138–139; praises May
Reed 139; attends Tree's funeral 139–140;
and auction at His Majesty's 140; marries
and divorces Cyril 145; subsequent
career and death 146–147
Truman, General William (Olivia's father)
xi, 9; marriage and birth of sons xii;

birth of Olivia xi, xiii; meets long-term
mistress xiii; general assessment xviii;
becomes Inspector-General of Remounts
in Boer War xix; subject of public
inquiry xix, 22; admires Tree in *Business
is Business* 25; death 22, 30, 32
Twelfth Night (Shakespeare) 6

Ulysses (Stephen Phillips) 6, 9, 22, 38
Uniacke, Colonel Harry 115, 123, 127,
128, 129, 130, 131, 134, 139, 140, 143
Uniacke, Mrs 115, 123, 127, 128, 130,
132
Unruh, General von 51

Valpy, Beatrice 90, 91, 121, 123
Valpy, Oliver 90, 91, 92, 121, 130
Van Dyck, The (adapted by Cosmo Gordon
from the French of Eugène Fourrier
Peringue) 71
Victoria, Princess 17
Victoria, Queen 7
Vision of Delight, The (Ben Jonson) 104

Waller, Lewis 3, 141; and Maud Tree 3,
39, 65–66
Whistler, James MacNeill xvii
Wigram, Major Cyril 95; meets Olivia 79;
and a job with Tree 80, 81; Tree's doubts
about him 81–82; first marriage 96;
meets Olivia again 131; war career 134;
court-martialled 138; with Olivia as she
hears of Tree's death 138; marries Olivia
145; and is divorced 145
Wilde, Oscar xvi, 60, 74
Wilhelm II, Kaiser 51, 70, 128
Wiltshire, Barbara (Olivia's maid) 41, 70,
71, 72, 107, 121, 131; goes to India with
Olivia 93; and to Paris 99; subsequent
life with Olivia and Isolde 145–146
Winter's Tale, The (Shakespeare) 51, 52,
58, 60, 61, 65
Woman of No Importance, A (Oscar Wilde)
72, 74
Wood, Sir Evelyn 7
Wyndham, Sir Charles 104

You Never Can Tell (Bernard Shaw) 54, 73